AF606922

EVEREST 24

Published in the United States and Canada
by Smithsonian Books

Commissioning editor: Jason Hook
Managing editor: Slav Todorov
Consultant editors: Jamie Owen and Julie Cole
Project manager: Kathleen Steeden
Project editor: Caroline West
Designer: Luke Herriott

This book may be purchased for educational, business, or sales promotional use. For information, please write to: Special Markets Department, Smithsonian Books, P.O. Box 37012, MRC 513, Washington, DC 20013

ISBN: 9781588347824

Library of Congress Cataloging-in-Publication Data
available upon request.

Printed in Slovakia, not at government expense
28 27 26 25 24 1 2 3 4 5

Rolex supports the Society's Picture Library – with its unique images of Everest – and contributes towards conservation of the Society's Collections.

Royal Geographical Society
Enterprises

Commercial activities
supporting the charity

Smithsonian Books
Washington, DC

CONTENTS

6 Foreword

8 Preface

10 Introduction

14 Timeline

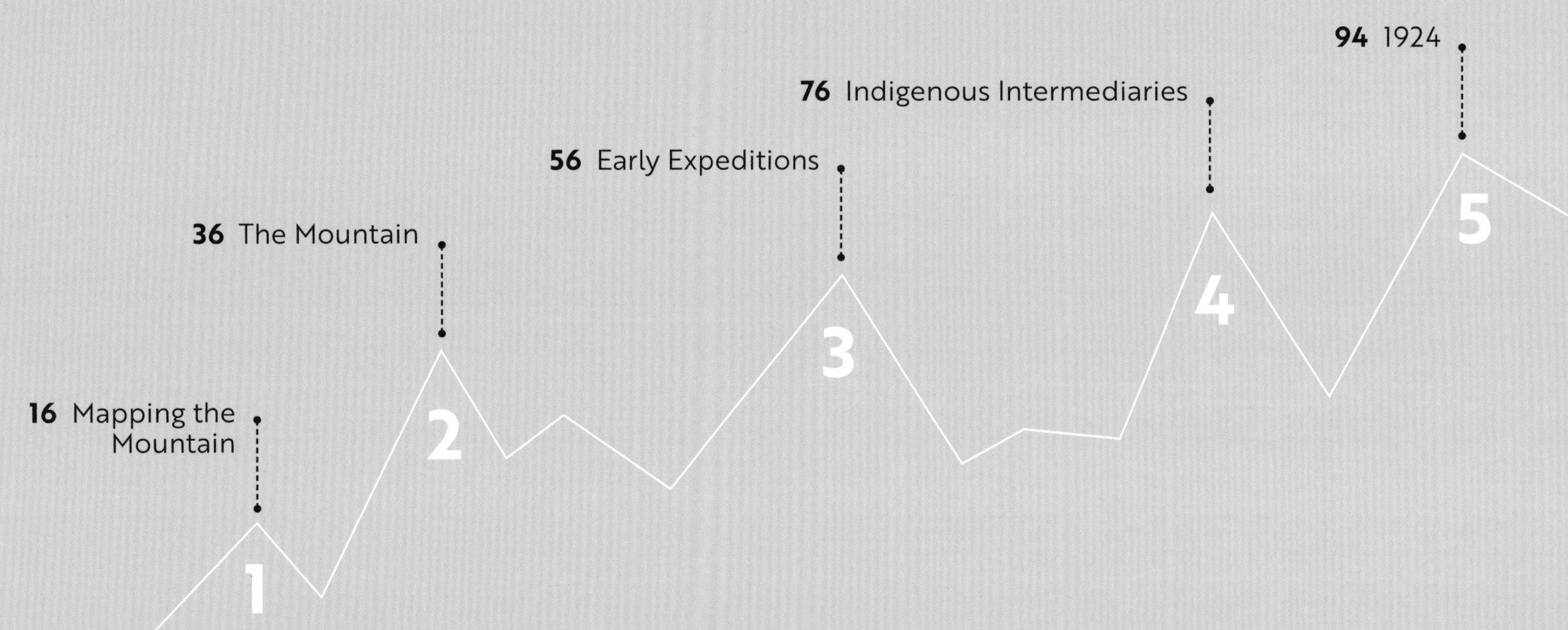

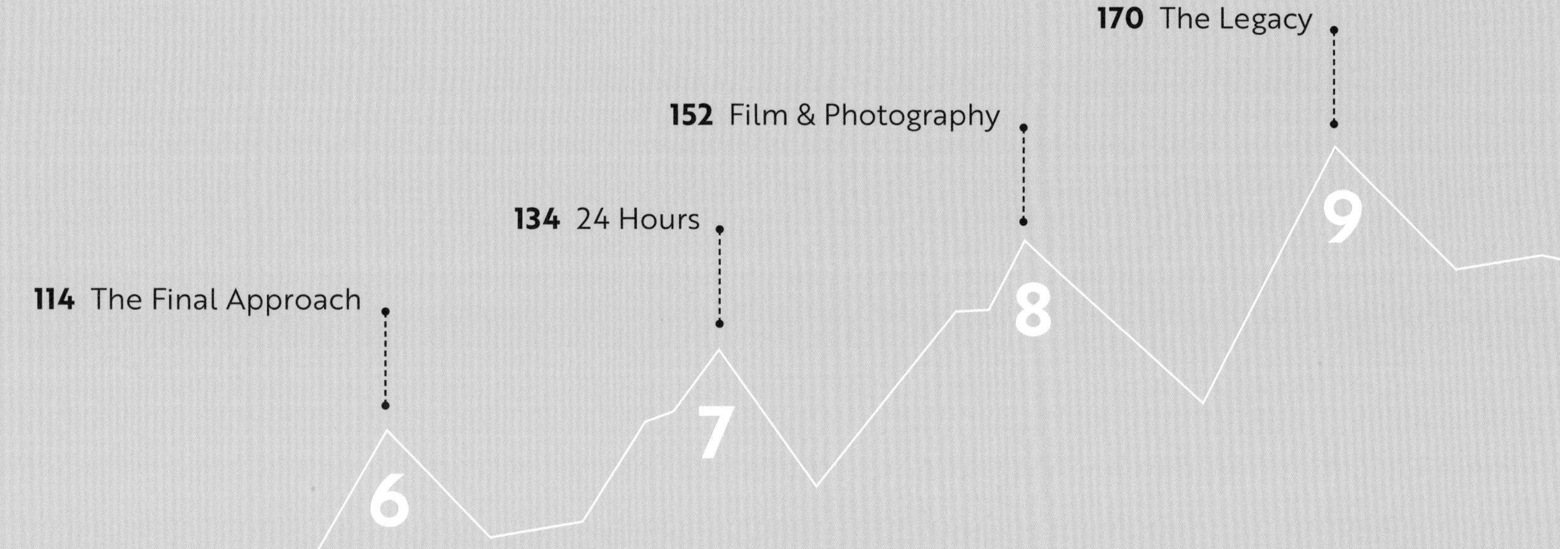

114 The Final Approach

134 24 Hours

152 Film & Photography

170 The Legacy

186 Afterword

188 Select Bibliography

190 Index

192 Acknowledgements

FOREWORD

by Norbu Tenzing

One hundred years since the disappearance of George Mallory and Andrew Irvine, and just over 70 years after the historic ascent of Mount Everest on 29 May 1953, we have an iconic and enduring image of my father, Tenzing Norgay, on the summit holding aloft the four flags of Great Britain, Nepal, India and the United Nations in his right hand. The image inspires not only Sherpas, but also those who embrace the spirit of mountaineering.

Since the early Everest expeditions of the 1920s, Sherpas, Tibetans, Bhotiyas and other Indigenous communities have been essential for helping the "sahibs" get their supplies to Base Camp and beyond. In 1929, the Himalayan Club – formed "to encourage and assist Himalayan travel and exploration, and to extend knowledge of the Himalaya and adjoining mountain ranges through science, art, literature and sport" – began issuing little red porter books in which expedition leaders could describe the work and character of an individual. These then served as a résumé/recommendation for future expeditions. The first entry in my father's red book, on 14 July 1936, was by Hugh Ruttledge, the leader of the 1936 Mount Everest Expedition. He wrote: "Character excellent, Warrens servant". The entries in my father's red book grew over time, with many still erroneously referring to him as simply "porter and personal servant". Indeed, even as Sherpas gained experience on the mountain and earned a name for themselves for their hard work, dedication and loyalty, the relationship between Sherpa men and the "sahibs" was unmistakably colonial, with Sherpas placed in a subservient role to the exploratory aspirations of the Westerners.

It was only in the early 1950s that the role of Sherpas began to shift. Highly qualified and experienced Sherpas, like my father, did not see themselves as porters and rightfully demanded to become fully fledged members of the expedition. The following decades also saw other changes in Himalayan mountaineering. The combination of Nepal opening its borders and the rapid advances in equipment attracted world-class climbers to the Himalayas. New, bold and challenging ascents, including climbing without oxygen, skiing down Everest and speed records, were established. While the spirit of exploration flourished in the 1980s, Sherpas were seldom acknowledged for their contributions. Their names did not even appear while setting major mountaineering records or when they died.

Mountaineering is the primary, and sometimes only, source of income for many Sherpas. The risks facing high-altitude mountaineering workers have always been high, with life-changing consequences to the family of those killed or disabled due to a mountaineering accident. My father advocated for their protection throughout his mountaineering career, but it is an issue which still persists today.

The commercialization of Everest in the 1990s changed things. Now, as Sherpas are forced to find a delicate balance between helping their clients while proving themselves by achieving record ascents, a group of highly qualified Sherpa men and women have begun to emerge as true leaders. As a result, the Everest narrative is gradually falling under the control of Sherpas, both on and off the mountains. Educated and entrepreneurial Sherpas began to operate expeditions on their own, cutting into the monopoly of foreign operators. Today, we see increasing competition among tour operators (both local and foreign), which results in a transactional atmosphere. The relationship between Sherpas offering high-altitude mountaineering and the paying climbers has shifted from one of friend/guest to client/service provider.

The aftermath of the 2014 Everest avalanche, which killed 16 Sherpas (leaving 52 children without fathers), marked another turning point. It led Sherpas on the mountain and in the wider diaspora to protest against poor wages and bad conditions for the first time. The images of Sherpas advocating for their rights was shocking to a world that was so used to seeing Sherpas smiling gratefully.

The dawn of the internet and social media has had an irreversible impact on the Himalayan mountaineering industry as new kinds of thrill-seekers, the "Instagrammers", have made their way to Everest. Chomolungma, as we Sherpas and Tibetans call Everest, has become "Everest Inc.", with highly skilled Sherpas being forced to prove themselves with ever greater world records.

One hundred years since George Mallory's final summit attempt, the fascination with Everest continues. However, the conditions in which mountaineers find themselves on the mountain are not the same; the snow and ice are melting at a rapid rate. The latest scientific reports claim that 80 per cent of Hindu-Kush-Himalayan glaciers will disappear by 2100 if humanity continues on its current global carbon emissions pathway. The number of people flocking to the summit also continues to rise, with the waste left behind by the expedition teams accumulating, seeping into the land and water systems.

Responsible tourism, improved working conditions for high-altitude mountaineering workers, and the enforcement of sustainable waste management practices can help lessen the impact on the environment. A collective effort is now essential to preserve the sacred and once pristine "roof of the world" for future generations: mountaineers must choose to climb responsibly, respect the mountain and its communities, and reduce their impact on its delicate ecosystem, while recognizing and appreciating the work of Sherpas in helping them achieve their dream of scaling the world's highest mountain.

PREFACE

The Royal Geographical Society (with the Institute of British Geographers) is the UK's learned society and professional body for geography. We advance geography and support geographers in the UK and across the world through research and education.

Our internationally recognized Collections contain over two million items with examples of photography stretching back to the inception of the medium as well as the largest private map collection in the world. One of the most important archives within this wider Collection is that relating to the nine British Mount Everest expeditions from 1921 to 1953. These collections contain over 18,000 photographs and a huge volume of written material, from planning documents to expedition reports and correspondence.

The Everest expeditions have quite often been cast as Western men battling against the unknown in testing climatic conditions to conquer the highest peak in the world. But that's far from the only narrative shown by our archive. Over the last two decades, the RGS has opened this archive and actively sought to engage with academics to carefully examine these important historical documents. What comes to startling light are the "hidden histories" – the stories of Indigenous Himalayans and those from elsewhere in the region who through their own physical labour or expertise supported the expeditions and made them successful. This work also expands our knowledge of the scientific advances but also the politics that lay behind these ventures.

The essays featured in this book highlight some of the rich and insightful research that has been undertaken on our Everest archives in recent years in relation to the 1924 expedition. I hope you enjoy learning about some of these incredible new perspectives in *Everest 24: New Views on the 1924 Mount Everest Expedition*.

Professor Joe Smith

Director
Royal Geographical Society (with IBG)

On the evening of 10 March 1919, a confident young army officer made an intriguing presentation at the Royal Geographical Society. John Noel described a clandestine journey he had undertaken through Sikkim and Tibet six years earlier. Travelling in disguise, he set out to identify the passes that lead to Everest and reached a point 40 miles from the mountain. Only the summit was visible, but this was the closest a Westerner had ever been to the peak.

Noel's talk stimulated new momentum for an Everest expedition, and in early April 1920 a joint committee was formed between the RGS and the Alpine Club. The Himalayan Committee agreed that the RGS would lead the expedition to Base Camp and map the surrounding region with the Alpine Club providing the expertise and personnel for climbing the mountain itself. This combined endeavour resulted in nine Everest expeditions, leading to the first ascent in 1953.

The first two expeditions in 1921 and 1922 were instrumental in identifying the equipment, logistics and climbing strategy required to reach the summit. But it is the third expedition in 1924 that is most remembered. The team was incredibly persistent, and after months of high winds, the weather finally settled just ahead of the approaching monsoon. Climbing alone, Edward Norton reached an altitude of 28,126ft (8,573m), and four days later George Mallory and Andrew Irvine disappeared upwards into the clouds as they were climbing high on the Northeast Ridge. They were never seen alive again, and there has been endless speculation ever since as to whether they reached the summit or not.

Everest was eventually climbed from Nepal via the Southeast Ridge in 1953 by an expedition led by John Hunt. And two years later, another British expedition climbed Kanchenjunga (28,169ft/8,586m) for the first time. The Himalayan Committee was no longer required, but the 1953 expedition had made a significant profit, which was used to set up the Mount Everest Foundation. This charity funds hundreds of exploratory mountaineering and scientific expeditions across the world, being jointly administered by the RGS and the Alpine Club.

This book celebrates the vision, determination and ambition of those taking part in this extraordinary endeavour a century ago and is brought to life by the enduring mystery of Mallory and Irvine. But above all it highlights the remarkably successful partnership between the RGS and the Alpine Club that ultimately led to the first ascents of two of the three highest mountains on Earth.

Simon Richardson

President
Alpine Club

INTRODUCTION

Welcome to *Everest 24: New Views on the 1924 Mount Everest Expedition*, the publication of which has been timed to coincide with the centenary of this now famous expedition.

The 1924 Mount Everest Expedition was an incredibly important moment in the history of Himalayan mountaineering. It was the culmination of two prior expeditions and cemented a global public fascination with the mountain, which at 29,032ft (8,849m) is the tallest in the world. The unparalleled coverage of the 1924 expedition – memorably captured on film by the official photographer John Noel and shown across the world in the resulting feature film *The Epic of Everest* – combined with the drama surrounding the disappearance of George Mallory and Andrew Irvine, placed the mountain squarely in the Western public mind.

To the mountaineering community in Europe and North America, climbers such as George Mallory, Andrew Irvine, Noel E. Odell and T. Howard Somervell were climbing into the unknown, such was Western ignorance of the region at the time. And they were doing so using pioneering new technology in some of the most difficult weather, temperatures and altitude conditions on Earth. Yet there was also another side to the expedition. The mountain was far from unknown to the Tibetan, Sherpa, Bhotiya and other ethnicities who called the Himalayan region home and the mighty mountain "Miti guti cha-phu long-nga" or Chomolungma (meaning "Goddess Mother of the World"). For those living in the shadow of the mountain it was an object of reverence and a source of spirituality. Thus, when the British expeditionary teams arrived in Tibet a delicate balance had to be maintained between the desire to climb and showing respect for the Indigenous communities and the spiritual significance of the mountain. Indeed, without the knowledge and direct assistance of these local communities George Mallory and Andrew Irvine would never have been able to attempt the summit. Given the cultural attitudes of the time it was always going to be difficult to maintain a degree of balance.

In this book we present a newly curated selection of original photographs taken during the expedition, including hand-coloured lantern slides by John Noel, the expedition cinematographer, and rarely seen black-and-white photographs by Bentley Beetham. Also featured are contemporary maps of the region, correspondence from the expedition and a selection

1. "At the North Col". This photograph shows expedition members, including Sherpas, resting in the snow during their climb of the North Col, the lowest point of one of the three ridges that lead to Everest's summit. Photographed by J. B. Noel for the 1924 Mount Everest Expedition.

1

of fascinating images of artefacts, all brought together in one volume to tell the incredible story of the 1924 expedition.

To support the photographs from the expedition archives we also feature additional images that show historical events and important figures to lend context to the expedition, drawing on the early photographic work of Himalayan pioneer Alexander Kellas and the stunning images of John Claude White, a British diplomat working in the region at the time.

The items you see in this book are all held within the Collections of the Royal Geographical Society (with IBG). As one of the key partners in the expedition, along with the Alpine Club of London, the Society holds over 18,000 photographs from the nine British Mount Everest expeditions from 1921 to 1953, which form part of a wider collection of international significance.

Drawing on the full breadth of the images from the Society's collection, and not only those relating to the 1924 expedition itself, the book attempts to set the expedition in its historical context (the British authorities hoped that attainment of the summit would be a source of national prestige and affirm Britain's global position) and to understand why it is considered so important. It also aims to draw attention to the stories and invaluable contribution of the Indigenous intermediaries – the translators, negotiators, officials, porters and climbers – without whom the expedition just would not have been possible.

Although our approach to the telling of the story is chronological, we have overlaid the narrative with commissioned essays by leading experts in order to examine the role of the Indigenous participants, the geopolitical situation at the time, and how the expedition was documented on camera and film, as well as the resulting legacy of the expedition. Each chapter starts with a short introduction, leads into an essay by an expert author and a gallery of some of the expedition's most stunning and important images, and then concludes with a "From the Collections" feature that considers a particular topic or photographer of interest.

We very much hope you enjoy this book – a celebration of the heroism, determination and indomitable spirit of all involved in the attempt on Mount Everest in 1924.

2. "Tent amongst ice-pinnacles". Due to blizzard conditions and severe cold temperatures, the 1924 expedition struggled to establish a camp at the North Col, weakening the party and delaying their summit attempts. Photographed by J. B. Noel for the 1924 Mount Everest Expedition.

2

TIMELINE

1903–4
Colonel Francis Younghusband leads an expedition into Tibet that is effectively a temporary invasion by British Indian armed forces.

1909
American Robert E. Peary claims to have reached the North Pole (with Matthew Henson and the Inuit Ootah, Egigingwah, Seegloo and Ooqueah).

14 December 1911
Norway's Roald Amundsen wins the race to the South Pole (with Olav Bjaaland, Helmer Hanssen, Sverre Hassel and Oscar Wisting).

17–18 January 1912
Britain's Captain Robert Falcon Scott and his companions (Edward Wilson, Edgar Evans, Lawrence Oates and Henry Bowers) reach the South Pole but die on the return journey.

1921
The British 1921 Mount Everest Reconnaissance Expedition, including George Mallory, reaches the North Col at 23,000ft (7,010m), identifying a potential route to the summit.

1922
The 1922 Mount Everest Expedition, including Mallory, reaches 27,300ft (8,321m) using supplementary oxygen; the porters Lhakpa, Narbu, Pasang, Pemba, Sange, Temba and Antarge die in an avalanche.

1924 Mount Everest Expedition
George Mallory and Andrew Irvine vanish on the final ascent, leaving the enduring mystery of whether they reached the summit. The expedition also claims the lives of Man Bahadur and Lance-Naik Shamsherpun.

1933
The 1933 Mount Everest Expedition attains an altitude of 28,120ft (8,571m).

1933
Irvine's ice-axe is found on the north face of Everest.

1935
The 1935 Mount Everest Expedition, designed as a reconnaissance expedition for the 1936 expedition and with Tenzing Norgay in the party, summits a number of lesser peaks.

1936
The 1936 Mount Everest Expedition is hampered by bad weather and an avalanche.

1938
The 1938 Mount Everest Expedition is defeated by bad weather in its attempts to reach the summit.

1951
The 1951 Mount Everest Reconnaissance Expedition surveys a new route for climbing Everest via Nepal and the southern face.

1952
During the Swiss Mount Everest Expedition, Raymond Lambert and Tenzing Norgay achieve an altitude of 28,199ft (8,595m).

29 May 1953
In the 1953 British Mount Everest Expedition, Edmund Hillary (New Zealand) and Tenzing Norgay (Nepal) become the first confirmed climbers to reach the peak of Everest.

1975
Junko Tabei (Japan) becomes the first woman to reach the summit of Everest.

1978
Reinhold Messner (Italy) and Peter Habeler (Austria) become the first climbers to summit Everest without supplementary oxygen.

1988
Lydia Bradey (New Zealand) becomes the first woman to summit Mount Everest without supplementary oxygen.

1999
The Mallory and Irvine Research Expedition discovers the body of George Mallory at 26,760ft (8,156m).

2003
Sibusiso Emmanuel Vilane (Swaziland) becomes the first black person to summit Mount Everest.

2019
Saray Khumalo (Zambia) becomes the first black African woman to summit Mount Everest.

1

MAPPING THE MOUNTAIN

The Himalayan range, a mountain chain containing more than 100 peaks over 24,000ft (7,300m), stretches from the plains of the Indian subcontinent to the Tibetan Plateau. It began forming over 40 million years ago when the Indian subcontinent collided with Eurasia and the Himalayan mountains rose in earnest around 20 million years ago. The Great Himalayan Range, about 1,400 miles long and containing Everest itself, probably became the highest mountains on Earth only within the last 600,000 years.

This imposing mountainous chain is at once both a significant barrier to human travel and commerce and one of the world's most beautiful and dramatic regions. Surveying and mapping this complex landscape has been attempted over a long and sustained period for many reasons: Tibet's central geographical position, bordered by China, India, Nepal, Sikkim and Bhutan, lends it strategic importance, but its mountainous landscape also captivates in its own right.

However, charting an area the size of the Himalayan range on foot, with such complex geography, an ever-changing political landscape, competing international interests and extremes of climate, was never going to be a simple endeavour.

Mapping the Himalayas has been undertaken by many nations over time and in many ways. Comparing the first European printed map, produced by Jean-Baptiste Bourguignon D'Anville and published in 1733 (image 4, page 21), with a tracing of a striking Tibetan pictorial map predating 1898 (image 7, page 25) highlights the different approaches to mapping the region and the differing purposes behind doing so.

This chapter also presents images that show the concerted effort made by the British, with support from Tibetans, Sherpa and Ghurkas, in the 1920s to map the mountain for climbing. We see, for example, Henry T. Morshead with Gujjar Singh plane-tabling (image 3, opposite), mapping the area in painstaking mathematical detail. Their work was then augmented by Edward O. Wheeler's photographic survey, which pinpointed the exact shapes of the mountains (image 12 page 31). With each passing year this international endeavour brought the geography of Everest into greater resolution.

"I begin to look forward to the day when glaciers will no longer be represented, as they were on the early Indian or Caucasian surveys, without their heads or tails – that is, without their névés or their moraine-cloaked lower portions, or with rivers rising above them and flowing through them. In time perhaps every closet cartographer will recognize that glaciers do not lie along the tops of lofty ridges, but descend in to valleys."

– Douglas Freshfield, "On Mountains and Mankind", Presidential Address to the Geographical Section at the Cambridge Meeting of the British Association, 1904

3. Henry Morshead plane-tabling with Gujjar Singh (standing to his right) for the 1921 Mount Everest Reconnaissance Expedition. Morshead, who had previously attempted a climb of Kamet, a peak in India, with Scottish mountaineer Alexander Kellas in 1920, led the Survey of India team. Photographed by C. K. Howard-Bury and hand-tinted by J. B. Noel.

3

THE CARTOGRAPHIC STORY

Essay by Dr Katherine Parker

From their inception, Western encounters with the mountain now called Everest were intimately tied to visualizing and integrating it into the developing mapping of the region. To climb the mountain, one had to know it – its height, its approaches, its composition, crags and crevices. Recording the geography of Everest is a process that involved various individuals and continues to this day, thanks to the changeable nature of mountainous terrain and the alterations wrought by increased human interaction and climate change.

Tibetans, Sherpa, Bhotiya and people of different mountain ethnicities have known and interacted with the mountain for centuries, and it continues to hold a position of religious importance for local peoples. Tibetans knew the peak as Chomolungma, while it was Sagarmatha to the Nepalese. The Chinese were also familiar with the region; they surveyed the area (1708–16) and the mountain appears as part of a group called Jumu Lungma Alin on a Jesuit map (1717–18) based on these observations. French geographer and cartographer Jean-Baptiste Bourguignon D'Anville then integrated information from this survey into the first European map of the area, *Carte Générale du Tibet ou Bout-tan et des Pays de Kashgar et Hami* (1733).

The British were captivated by the High Himalayas, and particularly with precisely how high it was. James Rennell, Surveyor General of Bengal in the late eighteenth century, carried out a comprehensive survey of large parts of India in the 1770s and suggested that the mountain range was taller than the Andes, then considered the most substantial in the world. Rennell's survey led to the Great Trigonometrical Survey (GTS), an imperial project which sought to make South Asia physically and intellectually accessible to colonialists via a grid of precise measurements.

Labelled by Clements Markham, President of the Royal Geographical Society from 1893 to 1905, as "one of the most stupendous works in the whole history of science", the survey began its work in Madras, in 1802, under the leadership of British surveyor William Lambton. Lambton's interest was geodesy, the study of the precise shape of the Earth, and his aim was to measure its curvature by a process known as triangulation, whereby a baseline between two points, usually about 7 miles apart, was measured using a chain of precisely known length mounted on wooden trestles. Then, from each of the two points, the angle between the baseline and the sight-line to a third point was measured using a theodolite, a surveying instrument that measures both vertical and horizontal angles. George Everest, a young artillery officer, joined the GTS as assistant

4. The first European printed map of Asia from 1733 by Jean-Baptiste Bourguignon D'Anville. "Tchoumour Lancma" (that is, Chomolungma, the Tibetan name for Everest) appears as "Tchoumour lancma M." to the lower central edge of map (to the right of the scale cartouche, just north of 27th parallel north).

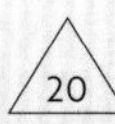

CARTE GENERALE
DU TIBET
OU BOUT-TAN
ET DES PAYS DE KASHGAR ET HAMI
DRESSÉE SUR LES CARTES ET MEMOIRES
DES RR PP JESUITES DE LA CHINE
et accordée avec la situation constante
de quelques Pays voisins
PAR LE Sr D'ANVILLE Geographe Ordre du Roi
Avril 1733.
COBI
DESERT DE SABLE
ECHELLE

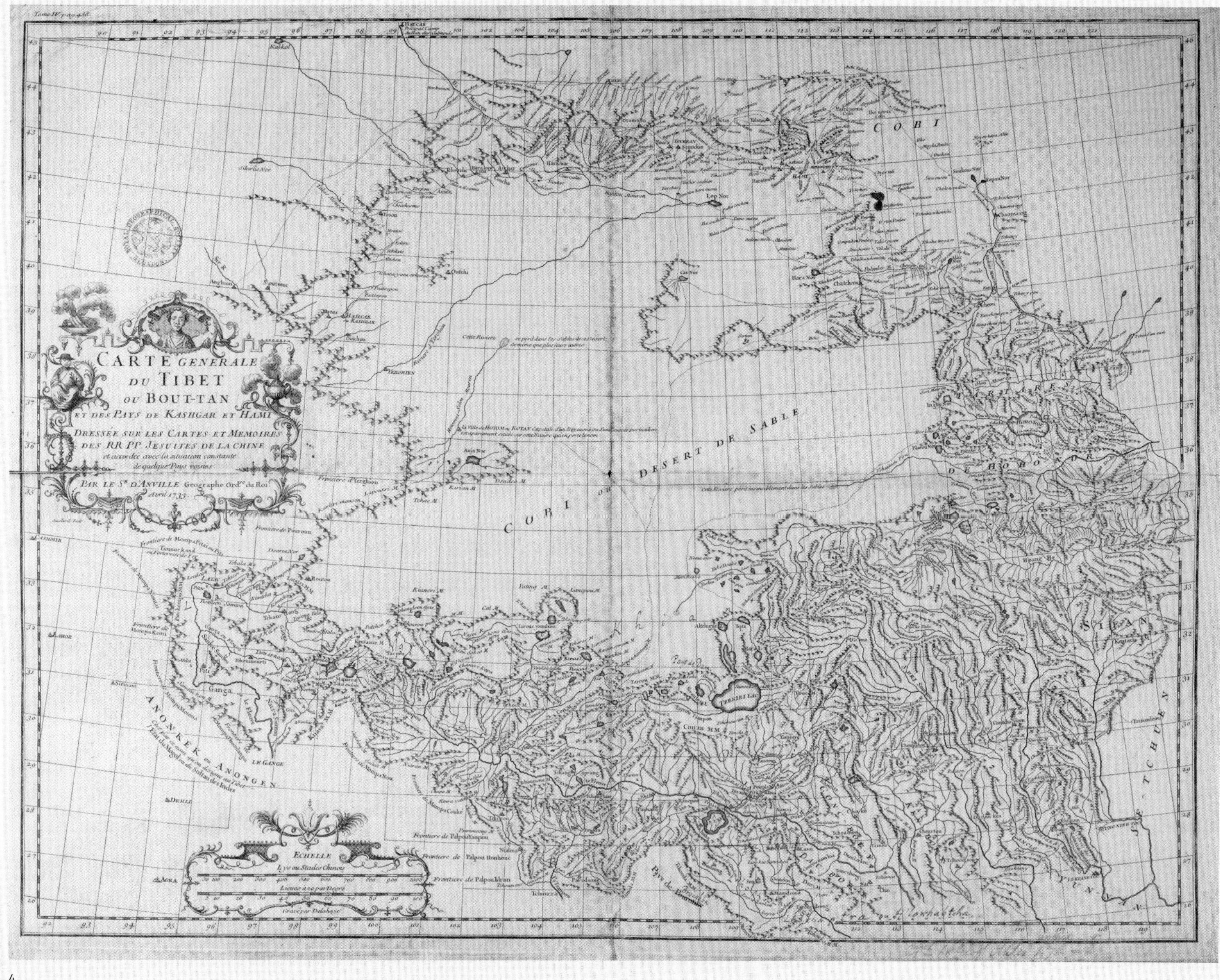

4

to Lambton in 1818, and on the death of Lambton in 1823 took over as Superintendent. He was later also appointed as Surveyor General of India. Everest continued Lambton's work and completed what became known as "Lambton's Great Arc", a geometric web of triangulations that ran the entire length of the Indian subcontinent to the Himalayas.

GTS surveyors would observe peaks from multiple stations, allowing them to claim with considerable accuracy which was the highest. Many of these surveyors and calculators were Indian in origin – known as pundits, they secretly explored regions north of British India. The chief computer Radhanath Sikdar, a Bengali, reported that their observations indicated that a little-known peak was probably the tallest in the world. The GTS surveyors numbered the plethora of mountains they saw and also attempted to learn their local names. For the highest, called Peak XV, their limited network missed references to a local name, however. This led Andrew Waugh to suggest in an 1856 letter to the President of the Royal Geographical Society, Sir Roderick Murchison, that the mountain identified by Sikdar carry the name of Everest, Waugh's predecessor and former Superintendent of the GTS.

The pundit surveyors of the GTS initially surveyed the Eastern Himalayas because Westerners were barred from much of the region. These highly trained Indians had to conduct survey work while trying to blend in as traders or lamas (holy men). For Everest, one of the most important of these surveyors was Hari Ram, who first circumnavigated the mountain without specifically noting it. Later, small groups of Europeans managed to approach the mountain and its surroundings. For example, in 1904, as part of the military expedition to Lhasa led by Sir Francis Younghusband, Charles Henry Dudley Ryder, Cecil G. Rawling, Frederick M. Bailey and Henry Wood surveyed the Kara La Pass, photographed the mountain and confirmed Everest's status as the highest peak in the world. The immediate environs of the mountain, however, remained unrecorded.

The first large-scale concerted effort to reconnoitre the mountain itself came in 1921, when the Dalai Lama gave permission for the mountain to be surveyed in anticipation of an attempted climb the following year. Led by Colonel Charles Howard-Bury, the expedition mapped an area the size of Switzerland, performing a general survey at four miles to an inch and a detailed survey of the approach at one mile to an inch. They were attempting, in Michael Ward's words, "one of the last great prizes of mapping and mountain exploration". The survey party of Lalbir Singh Thapa, Gujjar Singh, Turubaj Singh, Henry T. Morshead, Edward O. Wheeler,

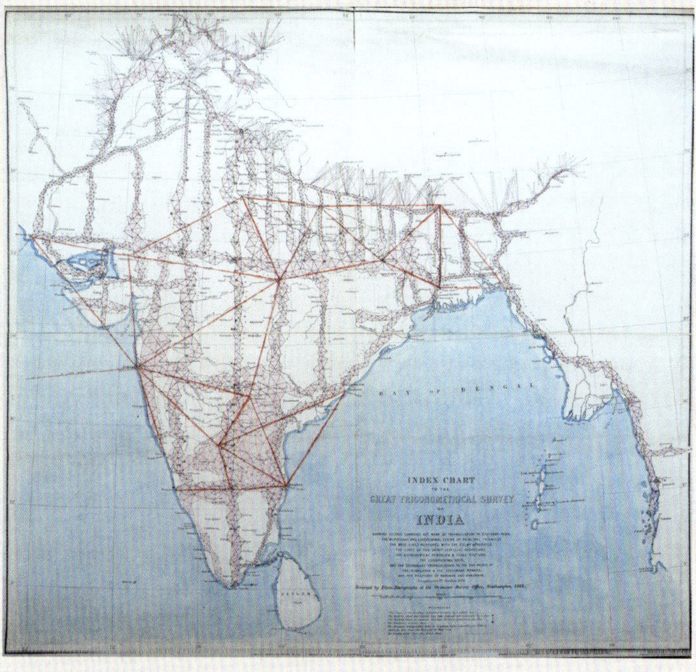

5

5. The 1870 Index Chart to the Great Trigonometrical Survey of India shows the extent of the survey from southern India to the Himalayan peaks. Running down the centre is the "Great Arc Series", often referred to as "Lambton's Great Arc", a geometric web of triangulations that ran the entire length of the subcontinent.

the photographer Abdul Jalil Khan and 16 porters took careful observations and records. They produced a high-resolution map in three sheets at one mile to an inch, showing the mountain's glaciers and possible routes to the top from the north, as well as a high-quality photographic collection.

The 1922 and 1924 expeditions both relied on and expanded the work of the 1921 Mount Everest Reconnaissance Expedition. Hari Singh Thapa was the surveyor on the 1924 Mount Everest Expedition, adding his own observations to that of his predecessors, as can be seen in the maps published in 1925 (see pages 32–33). In particular, he led surveys of the Gyachung Kang Glacier and the area east of the Rongbuk Monastery; he then surveyed the head of the West Rongbuk Glacier as well, in a team accompanied by skilled climber John de Vars Hazard. Examples of his hand-drawn contour sketch maps are in the Collections of the Society today, along with the printed maps to which he contributed.

Note. The Longitudes are referrible to the old value for the Madras Observatory 80°17'21"
to which a correction of − 3'25"5 is applicable to reduce to the value adopted by the
Admiralty and Royal Astronomical Society, or − 3'1"8 to reduce to the result of Taylor's
Observations up to 1830.
Heights brought up from the Sea Level at the Mouth of the Hoogly by Trigonometrical Levelling, and verified by extension of the operation to the Sea at Bombay & Kurachi.
The Peaks marked A. B. C. &c are identical with Colonel Crawford's Points and are so characterized by him.
W. H. Scott.
Chief Draftsman Su: G's Field Office
A. S. Waugh Lt Col.
S. Gl. of India
Scale 32 Miles to an Inch.
XV or MONT EVEREST 29002
XIII 27799
KATMANDU
DARJILING
IX or Kanchinjinga 28156
Bettiah
Segowlee
Durbungah
Purneah
J. F. Baness, Surveyor General's Field Office Dehra Doon 1857.

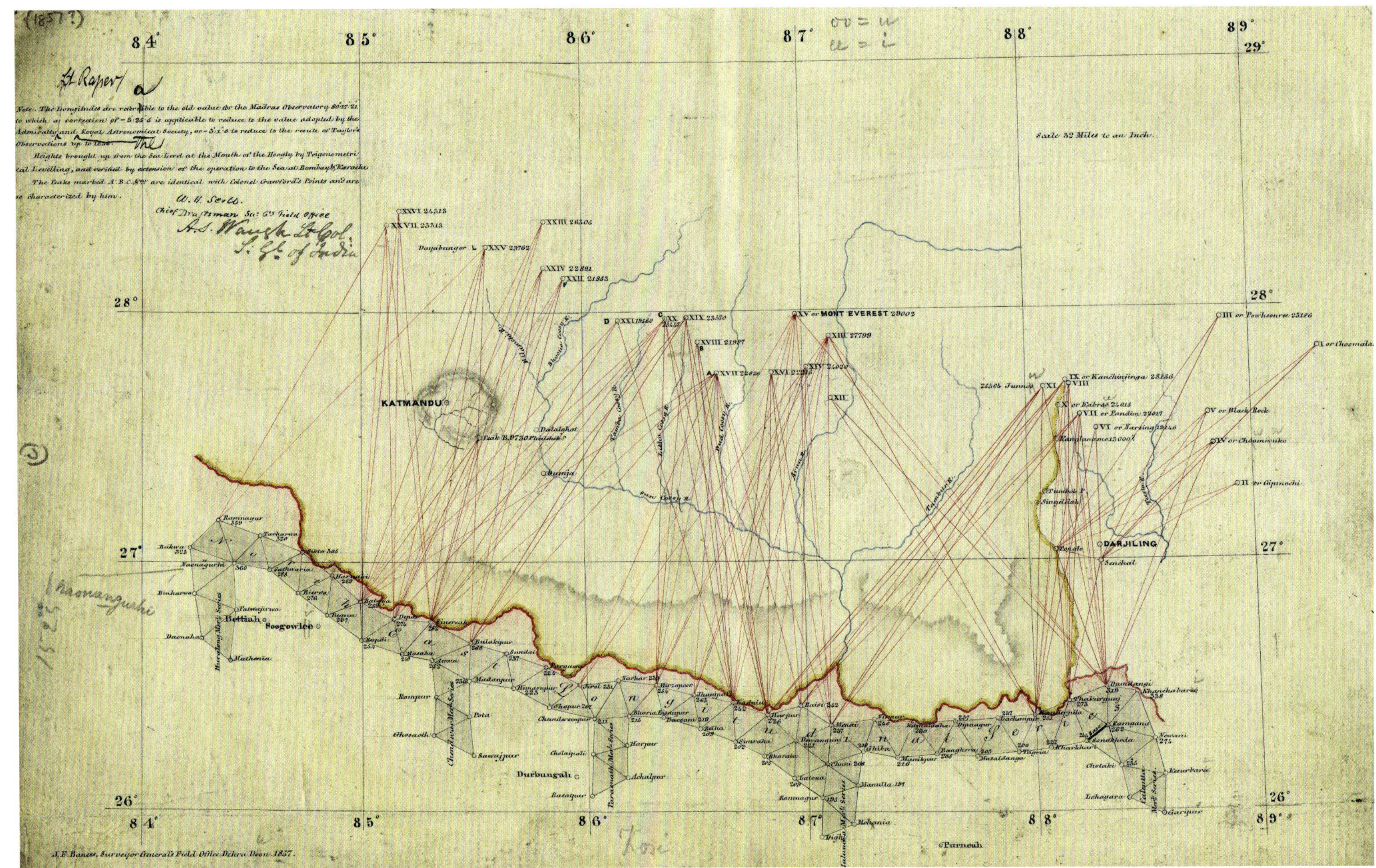

6

6. A map showing the triangulation of Peaks I to XXVII, including Mount Everest (Peak XV), to accompany a paper titled "On Mounts Everest and Deodanga" by Andrew Waugh, published in the *Proceedings of the Royal Geographical Society of London*, Volume 2 (1857–58).

7. A tracing from a photograph of a Tibetan pictorial map of the area around Mount Everest. The map was reproduced in *The Geographical Journal* in 1898 to accompany a paper by L. A. Waddell titled "The environs and native names of Mount Everest".

7

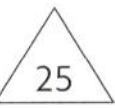

8

8. Lambton's Great Theodolite, used by William Lambton and George Everest during the Great Trigonometrical Survey of India. Weighing approximately half a tonne (about 500kg), it took 12 people to carry it. George Everest often praised the invaluable work of Syed Mir Mohsin Hussain, whose expertise in calibrating and repairing the instruments was vital to the success of the survey.

9. "Preliminary map showing original surveys made by Mt. Everest Detachment 1921". The part outlined in red to the centre-bottom of the map shows the area photo-surveyed by Edward O. Wheeler and his three Tibetan assistants, Gorang, Lagay and Ang Pasang.

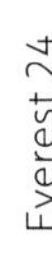

PRELIMINARY MAP showing original surveys made by
Mt EVEREST DETACHMENT 1921.
(Reproduced by Vandyke process from tracings made in the field.)
TRANS HIMALAYA RANGE
PHARUK
MOUNT EVEREST
SYMBOLS AND ABBREVIATIONS
Scale 1 inch = 4 miles.
Contours at 500 ft. vertical interval.
Note :- The area enclosed in red has been surveyed in detail by photographic method, and is only shown with approximate accuracy on this map.

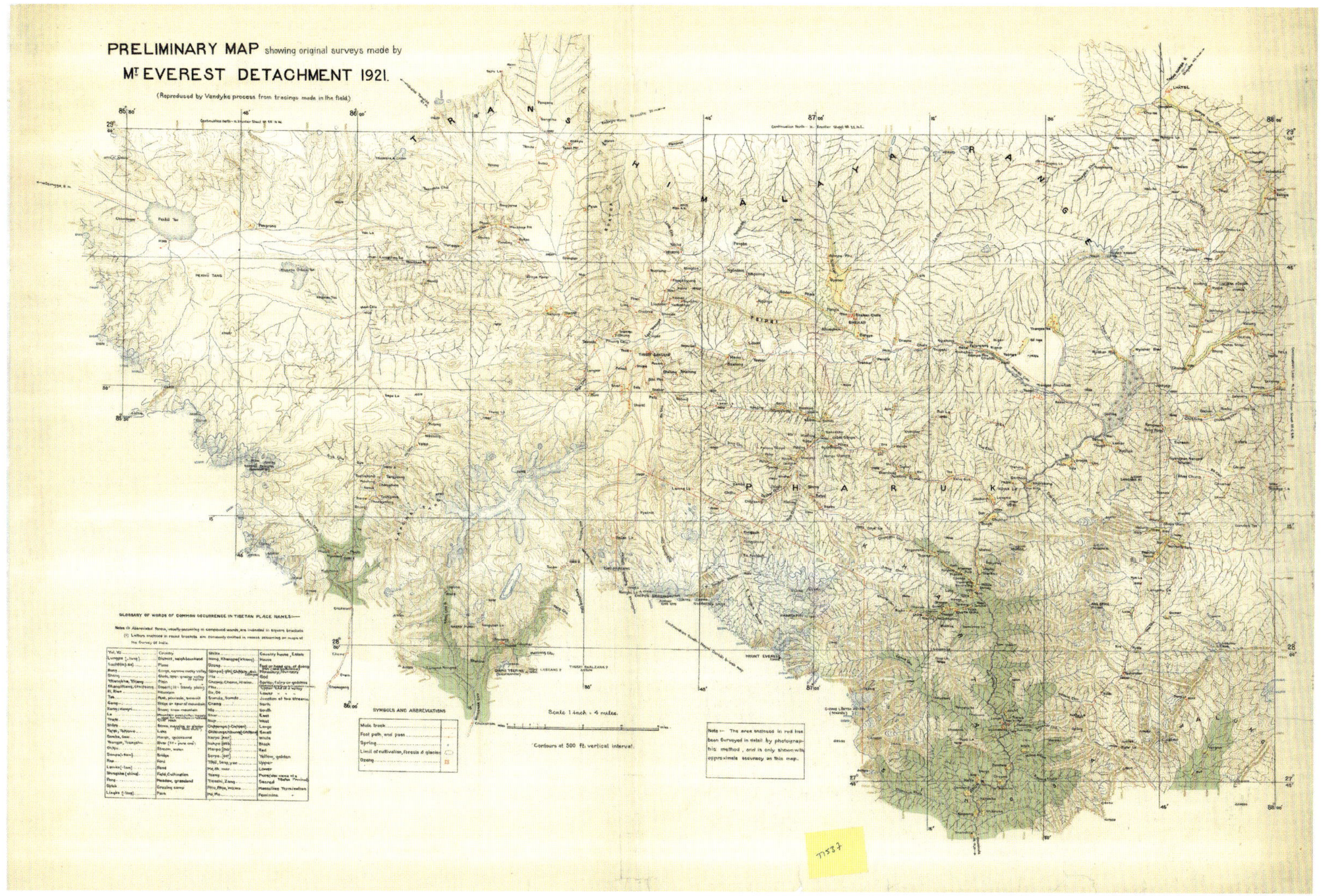

9

10

10. Three photographs taken by Edward O. Wheeler during the 1921 Mount Everest Reconnaissance Expedition, which combine to create a panorama of Mount Everest viewed from the East Rongbuk Glacier.

11

11. Edward O. Wheeler's photographic survey party, 1921 Mount Everest Reconnaissance Expedition. Using photo-topographical surveying instruments, Wheeler and his three Tibetan assistants, Gorang, Lagay and Ang Pasang, methodically photo-surveyed and mapped the immediate area around the approaches to Mount Everest. Photographed by A. F. R. Wollaston.

12. "Preliminary Map of Mount Everest constructed at the R.G.S. from photographs and sketches made by the Expedition of 1921". The red dots show the sites of the stations from which Charles Howard-Bury used a Kodak Panoram camera to create a series of panoramas.

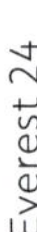

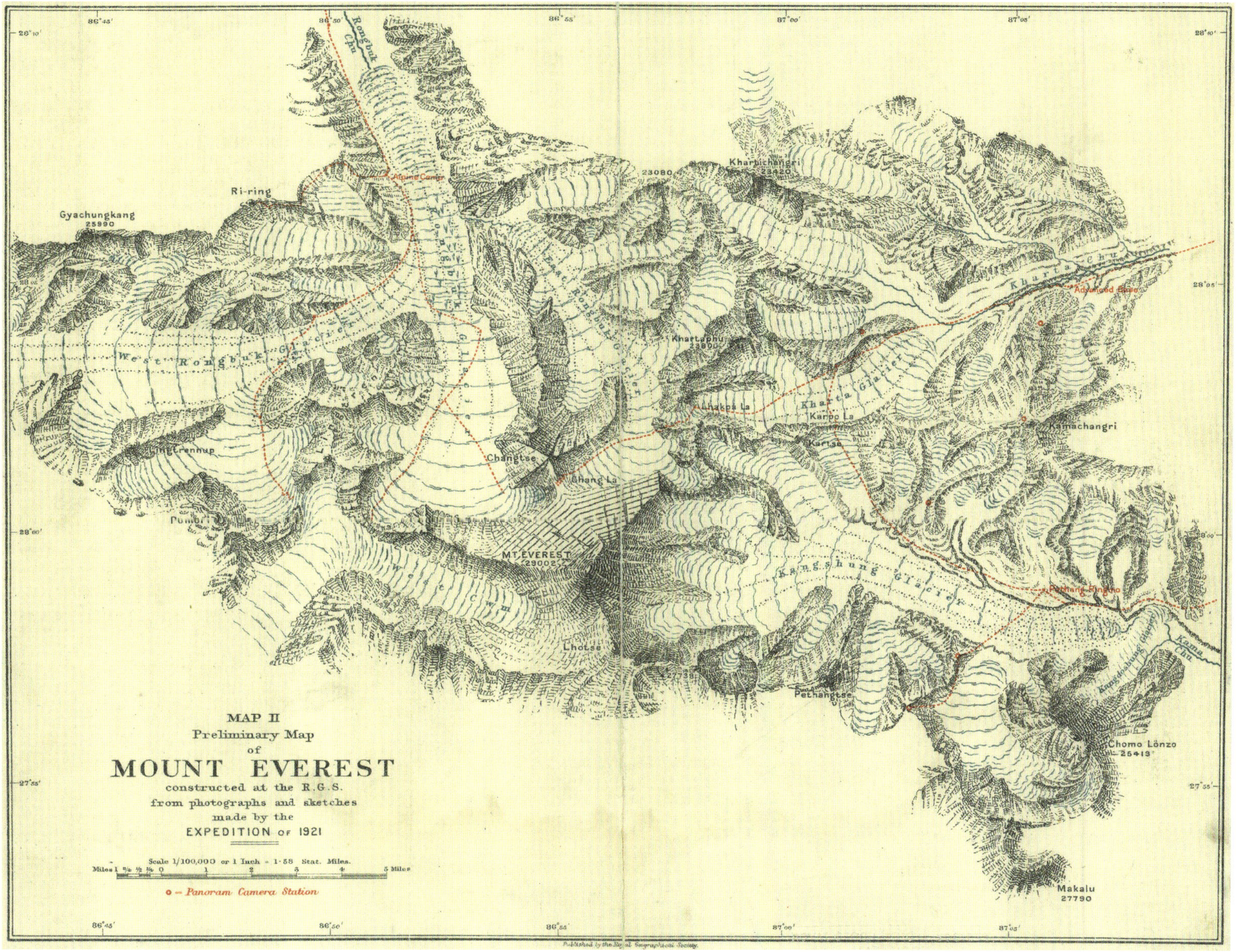

Gyachungkang
25990
Ri-ring
Alpine Camp
Rongbuk Chu
23080
Kharbichangri
West Rongbuk Glacier
Rongbuk Glacier
East Rongbuk Glacier
Khartaphu
Kharta Chu
Advanced Base
Kharta Glacier
Lhakpa La
Karpo La
Kamachangri
Changtse
Chang La
Pumori
MT. EVEREST
29002
West Cwm
Kangshung Glacier
Lhotse
Pethangtse
Kama Chu
Chomo Lönzo
25413
Makalu
27790

MAP II
Preliminary Map
of
MOUNT EVEREST
constructed at the R.G.S.
from photographs and sketches
made by the
EXPEDITION OF 1921

Scale 1/100,000 or 1 Inch = 1·58 Stat. Miles.
Miles 1 ¾ ½ ¼ 0 1 2 3 4 5 Miles

o = *Panoram Camera Station*

Published by the Royal Geographical Society.

12

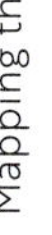

13

13. A tracing of the original surveys made by Hari Singh Thapa, an Indian surveyor who was attached to the 1924 Mount Everest Expedition.

14. "Mount Everest and the Group of Chomo Lungma. Drawn by Charles Jacot-Guillarmod from the photographic surveys of E. O. Wheeler for the Mount Everest Reconnaissance Expedition of 1921, with additions by Surveyor Hari Singh Thapa on the expedition of 1924, and from photographs of the three expeditions". Published by the Royal Geographical Society in 1925.

MOUNT EVEREST AND THE GROUP OF CHOMO LUNGMA
PART OF TIBET
DISTRICT OF THE DZONGPEN OF SHEKAR
PART OF NEPAL
MOUNT EVEREST
CHOMO LUNGMA
GYACHUNG KANG
PUMO RI
NUPTSE
LHO TSE
CHANG TSE
PETHANG TSE
KHARTI CHANG RI
Nup La
West Rongbuk Glacier
Far East Rongbuk Glacier
Kharti Changri Glacier
Kangshung Glacier
West Cwm Glacier
86°45′
86°50′
86°55′
87°0′
28°5′
28°0′
SCALE OF MILES
One Inch to One Mile, or 1:63,360
Contours are figured in Metres at 100-metre interval
Contours on Glaciers in blue
Glaciers are tinted pale blue.
Drawn by Charles Jacot-Guillarmod from the photographic surveys of Major Wheeler, R.E., Survey of India, on the Mount Everest Expedition of 1921, with additions by Surveyor Hari Singh on the Expedition of 1924, and from the photographs of the three expeditions. ¶ Reproduced for the Mount Everest Committee of the Royal Geographical Society and Alpine Club by the Ordnance Survey, 1925.
SCALE OF KILOMETRES
Heights are given in Metres and Feet 7032 (23070)
Points triangulated by Survey of India, thus
Camera Stations, thus
Intersected points, thus
Route and Camps in Red
ASIA S. 235
CHINA S. 306

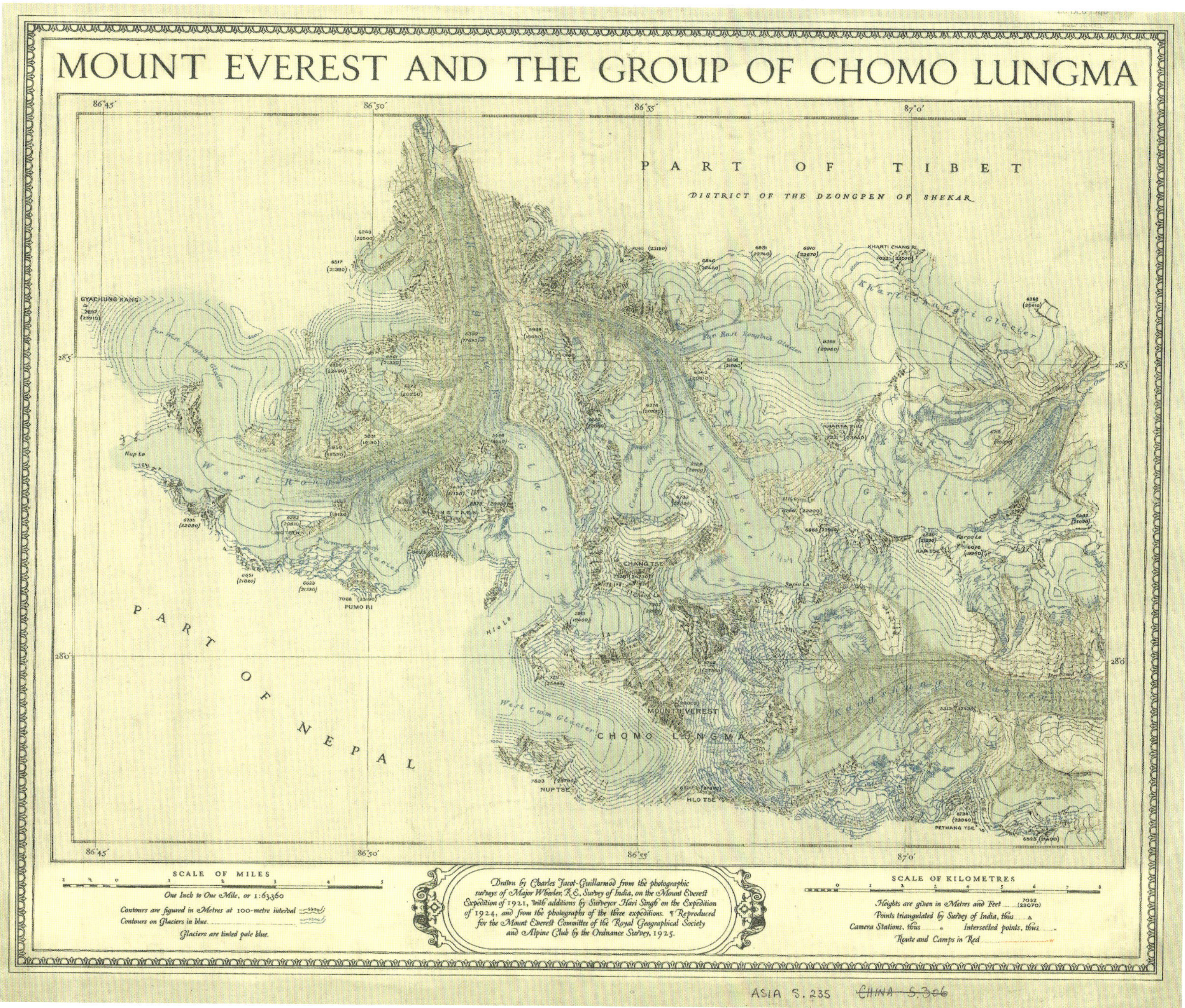

14

THE PUNDITS

From the collections

As the Great Trigonometrical Survey (GTS) reached the foothills of the Himalayas, the political climate of the time meant that access to the then independent kingdoms of Nepal, Sikkim, Bhutan, Assam, the North-East Frontier Agency and Tibet was not permitted. This left large blanks on the Survey of India maps of the Himalayan region. Strategic knowledge of the area was crucial to the British at that time in the political power play of the Great Game (the rivalry between the British and Russian empires over Central and South Asia).

Thomas Montgomerie, who joined the GTS in 1851, realized the solution lay in training the Indian workforce in surveying techniques. Disguised as traders or lamas (holy men), the pundits (from *pandit*, a Hindi word meaning "man of learning") learned to make observations without attracting the attention of the local authorities. They were trained to walk at exactly 2,000 paces to the mile and used a specially designed Buddhist rosary to keep count. They carried a Mani Kholo, or prayer wheel, to aid their disguise and hide their observations. The pundits travelled for months, sometimes years, and often through dangerous situations; many never returned.

One of the first pundits to explore Tibet was Nain Singh, a Bhotiya schoolmaster from Milam in northern Kumaon, Uttar Pradesh. During the years 1865–66, he walked approximately 1,200 miles and recorded the location of the Tibetan city of Lhasa, charted the course of the Tsangpo River, and mapped the Tibetan southern trade route. From 1874 to 1875, he travelled another 1,405 miles from Leh to Chetang. Other members of the Singh family also contributed to the exploration of the Himalayan region, including Nain Singh's cousin, Kishen Singh (code-named A-K). In an astonishing 2,800-mile journey he mapped the route north of Lhasa into Xinjiang. These lesser-known contributors to the Great Trigonometrical Survey of India not only helped to fill in the blanks on the maps but also provided valuable geographical and cultural knowledge of the region.

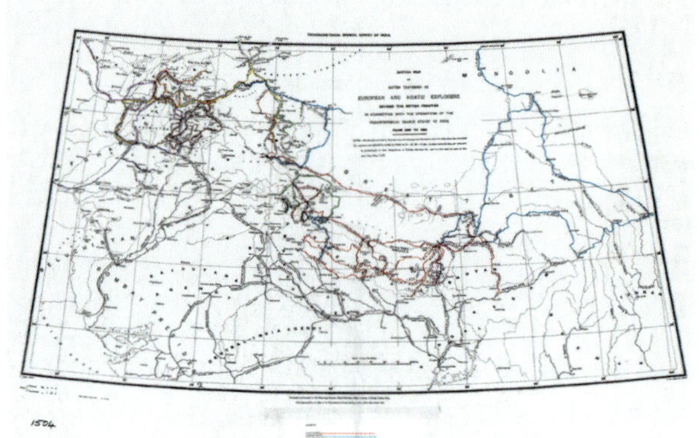

15

16

17

18

19

15. "Trans Frontier: Routes traversed by European and Asiatic Explorers beyond the British Frontier, in connection with the operations of the Trigonometrical Branch, Survey of India, from 1865 to 1883". This map shows the routes taken by the pundits Nain Singh, Kishen Singh, Kalian Singh, Mani Singh, the Mullah, the Havildar, the Mirza, Hari Ram and Sarat Chandra Das.

16. One of two sheets of a Survey of India map showing the route taken by Nain Singh "through Great Tibet from Ladakh to Assam" in 1874. The pundits' missions were shrouded in secrecy and each pundit was given a code name: Nain Singh's code names were "the Pundit", "the Chief Pundit" or "Number One".

17. The Pundit Sarat Chandra Das on a yak crossing the Donkhya Pass at 18,000ft (5,500m) in 1879. Born in Chittagong, East Bengal, Chandra Das studied civil engineering in Calcutta and worked as a headmaster for a Bhotiya boarding school in Darjeeling. Chandra Das's book *A Journey to Lhasa and Central Tibet* (1902) provided a detailed account of Lhasa and South Tibet.

18. Rai Bahadur Kishen Singh Milamwal, 1905. During his 1878–82 journey, Kishen Singh was robbed, imprisoned on suspicion of spying, and delayed for over a year in Lhasa while waiting for his caravan to leave. Photographer unknown.

19. A photogravure of Nain Singh who worked as a pundit for the Survey of India until his identity was revealed in 1876. He was awarded the Royal Geographical Society's Founder's Medal in 1877 "for his great journeys and surveys in Tibet and along the Upper Brahmaputra, during which he determined the position of Lhasa and added largely to our knowledge of the map of Asia".

2

THE MOUNTAIN

Mount Everest, standing at 29,032ft (8,849m), is on the border between Nepal and Tibet. There are many routes to the summit, but in the 1920s British attempts at climbing the mountain came exclusively from the north through Tibet because Nepal, bordered by India and China, remained closed to the outside world due to its policy of isolationism. Tibet remained a deeply religious society, with its leadership provided by the monasteries and the Dalai Lama. Britain and China vied with each other to gain influence over Tibet, which had a relationship with Britain through the latter's provision of arms to the Tibetan military.

British access to the mountain would be via the Rongbuk Monastery, founded in 1902, which for many Tibetans marked the sacred doorway to Everest. The monastery was also an important site of pilgrimage for Sherpas living in Nepal's Khumbu region, which added sensitive spiritual considerations to an already delicate political situation. At 16,434ft (5,009m) above sea level, the monastery sits at the northern end of the Rongbuk Valley, overlooking the Rongbuk Glacier, which is fed by the outflow of the East Rongbuk and West Rongbuk glaciers – a truly stunning and commanding position.

Among the many captivating images in this chapter you will see one of the oldest photographs of Mount Everest in the Society's collection: a panorama of the Himalayas showing the mountain photographed from Sandakphu, in Sikkim (image 23, pages 44–45). Although Everest's summit was still firmly out of reach, by 1921 expeditions were approaching the slopes of the mountain and gaining far greater clarity over the geographical details of Everest, as documented in A. F. R. Wollaston's stunning 1921 photograph (image 24, page 46). During these early expeditions, the teams also devloped a better understanding of the people and the monasteries they encountered, particularly the Rongbuk Monastery where they met Head Lama Dzatrul Rinpoche, as photographed by C. J. Morris in 1922 (image 31, page 53).

"Some day the political difficulties will be overcome, and a fully equipped expedition must explore and map Mount Everest."

– John Noel, Address to the Royal Geographical Society, March 1919

20. "Mount Everest in morning light, from camp at 22,500 ft", photographed by George Mallory during the 1921 Mount Everest Reconnaissance Expedition. In 1921, Mallory described his excitement and wonder at his first sight of Everest: "Gradually, very gradually, we saw the great mountain sides and glaciers and aretes, now one fragment and now another through the floating rifts, until far higher in the sky than imagination had dared to suggest the white summit of Everest appeared."

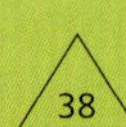

20

EVEREST AND THE FRONTIERS OF EMPIRE

Essay by Dr Jonathan Westaway

Following its confirmation as the world's highest mountain in 1856, Mount Everest was gradually incorporated into British imperial knowledge and governance via remote sensing, cartography and the imposition of new toponyms, a process that frequently obscured older Indigenous and regional topographies.

As an object of scientific and geostrategic interest, gathering knowledge of Mount Everest formed part of a wider project to render Asia governable by the British in India. The British constructed a narrative of discovery around the surveying of Everest that stressed its invisibility to Western ways of knowing and expressed considerable cartographic anxiety about blanks on the map in this sensitive border region. Even as late as 1921 Sir Francis Younghusband could still say: "we knew nothing of the immediate approaches to the mountain."

What these Western accounts failed to register was the visibility of Everest and its prominence in other ways of knowing, particularly those of Tibetan Buddhism. When Charles Howard-Bury was in Kalimpong, visiting the home of the local missionary, Dr J. A. Graham, he recorded a conversation with David Macdonald, the British Trade Agent in Yatung, Tibet, and the acting Political Officer, in Sikkim, at the time. Macdonald was Anglo-Sikkimese and fluent in the Tibetan language. Howard-Bury recorded: "He told me that an old Tibetan lama, who knew Mount Everest well, had described it as 'Miti guti cha-phu long-nga', 'the mountain visible from all directions, and where a bird becomes blind if it flies so high'."

For Tibetan and Nepalese Buddhists, the visibility of Everest was not merely physical; it was also informed by spiritual geographies, the summit being the abode of Miyolangsangma, the Goddess of Inexhaustible Giving and one of the Five Long-Life Sisters – a mountain deity still revered by Sherpas in the Solu-Khumbu region of Nepal today.

These competing narratives of invisibility and visibility highlight Mount Everest's status as a boundary object. The mountain is situated on the international border between Nepal and Tibet, both of which were closed to Western travellers in that period. Both countries were part of British India's geostrategic thinking, forming a section of an arc of "buffer states" the British hoped would exclude any influences from the Russian and Chinese empires, helping to secure the routes to India across the trans-Himalaya passes that might be used by invading armies.

Yet while Britain's relationship with Nepal was governed by treaty and the presence of a British Resident in Kathmandu from the early nineteenth

21

21. British guns being loaded at Chumbi, Tibet, during the British Mission to Tibet in 1903–4. Photographed by G. I. Davys.

century, ensuring the country was aligned with British foreign policy objectives, the position of Tibet caused the British Government of India considerable anxiety. Formally suzerain to the Chinese empire, Tibet acted with increasing autonomy in the late nineteenth century, as the Qing state's grip weakened on its western provinces. From the 1890s onwards, Britain's various proposals for climbing Everest, a peak located outside the British Empire, mirrored Britain's increasingly aggressive attempts to integrate Tibet more formally into British trade, security and political networks.

Younghusband first discussed the possibility of climbing Mount Everest with Charles Granville Bruce in 1893 when both were involved in a military mission to relieve the besieged British garrison in Chitral. Both men were to play critical roles in ensuring Tibet was opened up to British interests and Everest made accessible to British mountaineers. With Lord Curzon's appointment as Viceroy of India in 1899, the Government of India pursued a more aggressive "forward" policy with Tibet. Tibet's refusal to open diplomatic relations with British India saw Curzon send a punitive military mission to Lhasa in 1903–4, led by Younghusband.

The invasion of Tibet led to widespread bloodshed and wholesale looting of Tibetan cultural artefacts by British troops. Tibet's spiritual leader, the thirteenth Dalai Lama, fled to Mongolia. Britain imposed the 1904 Anglo-Tibetan Convention on Tibet, establishing the presence of British Trade Agencies in Yatung, Gyantse and Gartok and occupying the strategic Chumbi Valley after having imposed punitive reparations on Tibet. The Trade Agencies increasingly acted as intelligence-gathering centres under the jurisdiction of the British Political Officer in Sikkim. In 1910 the Chinese sent a military force

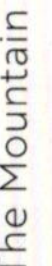

to Tibet to reassert their claim to political rule and the thirteenth Dalai Lama fled to Darjeeling in British India, where he came increasingly under the influence of Sir Charles Bell, the British Political Officer in Sikkim.

After the collapse of the Qing empire in 1911 and the expulsion of the Chinese from Lhasa, the Dalai Lama returned to Tibet. In January 1913 he reached Lhasa, issuing "what the Tibetans regard as a declaration for independence" from China. The Simla Convention of 1914 attempted to negotiate a tripartite agreement between Britain, Tibet and China that would fix international borders and define spheres of influence. Britain supported the idea of an "Outer Tibet" and "Inner Tibet", the former with a Tibetan administration in Lhasa, nominally suzerain to China but largely autonomous in its domestic and foreign policy – a position China could not accept. Early Republican China, however, was in no position to impose a settlement and withdrew from the convention. While the British and Tibetans proceeded with a bilateral agreement, the borders imposed at Simla became a long-standing cause of contention for successive Chinese administrations.

The British attempt to climb Mount Everest can be understood as a component of this British "forward" policy in Tibet. The Royal Geographical Society and the Alpine Club began lobbying the India Office and the Government of India in 1919 for permission to access Tibet, and by 1920 Sir Charles Bell had secured permission from the Dalai Lama for an expedition. In the post-war period, Everest took on an enhanced symbolic significance for the British imperial power. Characterized as the "Third Pole" and the last great challenge of the age of exploration, climbing Everest offered the British the opportunity to demonstrate their fitness to rule over British India by reasserting a form of imperial masculinity that had been shattered by the experiences of the First World War.

It was undertaken during a period of extreme geopolitical uncertainty, characterized by numerous threats to the borders of British India. The Anglo-Afghan war of 1919 had spilled over into full-scale tribal insurrection in the North-West Frontier Province, a conflict that lasted until 1923. Growing Soviet influence in Xinjiang and instability in Republican China threatened the borders of India just as Indian nationalists' increasing agitation for self-rule called into question the very legitimacy of the British Raj.

As the British Mount Everest Reconnaissance Expedition wound its way up the Chumbi Valley towards Everest in May 1921, Britain's influence in Tibet was at its zenith. Sir Charles Bell had been invited to Lhasa and was resident there from November 1920 to October 1921. Bell was the first European to arrive in Lhasa with an invitation from the Dalai Lama. Lord Curzon had become Foreign Secretary in 1919 and from 1921 the Foreign Office "declared that Britain would deal with Tibet as an effectively if not legally independent state". British military officers were training the Tibetan military in early 1923, as part of a broader strategy to support an autonomous Tibet with its own foreign policy and with the power to resist imposition of rule by China. But this high watermark of British influence in Tibet was short-lived. After the Mount Everest expedition of 1924 a number of issues led to a worsening of diplomatic relations between Tibet and Britain, some relating to the expedition itself. In 1924 the Tibetan government also believed it had evidence to suggest that F. M. Bailey, the British Political Officer in Sikkim, may have been involved in a plot to replace the Dalai Lama as head of state with the head of the Tibetan military, Tsarong Dzasa.

No British expedition to Everest was allowed back into Tibet until 1933 and no resident British diplomatic presence was allowed in Lhasa until 1936 (as explained in *The Legacy*, page 172). By 1947 Britain had quit India and any notion of Tibet as an autonomous entity was crushed by its forced reintegration into a resurgent China under the Chinese Communist Party in 1950–51.

22

22. "Chomolhari and Tibetan Camp near Phari". In 1920 Sir Charles Bell visited Lhasa seeking to obtain permission for the British to map and climb Everest. This picture shows Howard-Bury's camp on the Tibetan Plateau with Chomolhari in the distance. Photographed by C. K. Howard-Bury.

23

24

23. Previous page: "Mount Everest Range from Sandakphu". An early photograph taken around 1890 of Mount Everest and the Himalayan mountain range from Sandakphu in Sikkim. Photographer unknown.

24. "Everest from foot of Kharta Glacier". Mount Everest was known as Chomolungma to Tibetans, which means "Goddess Mother of the World". Photographed by A. F. R. Wollaston during the 1921 Mount Everest Reconnaissance Expedition.

25. "Kampa Dzong". The Everest expeditions of the early twentieth century passed the hilltop fort en route to Everest. It was here the expedition leaders would meet with local officials and change transport animals. Photographed by B. Beetham during the 1924 Mount Everest Expedition.

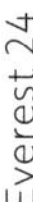

25

26

27

26. The Tibetan Buddhist wheel of life, known as "Bhavachakra", can often be found on the exterior of Buddhist temples and monasteries. The complex wheel is a symbolic representation of the Buddhist belief in cyclic existence and the continuous cycle of birth, life and death. Photographed for the 1924 Mount Everest Expedition and later hand-tinted by J. B. Noel.

27. A Tibetan mani chorten (a mound-like Buddhist shrine). Mani stones are stones, rocks or pebbles that are carved or inscribed with Buddhist prayers or scriptures, and often with the six-syllabled mantra "Om mani padme hum". The Tibetan porters would chant the "Om mani" incantation as they approached Everest. Photographed by B. Beetham.

28

28. "Inside the courtyard of Shekar Monastery". Photographed and later hand-tinted by J. B. Noel, 1924 Mount Everest Expedition.

29. "The Abbot of Shekar Chote". Photographed by C. K. Howard-Bury, 1921 Everest Reconnaissance Expedition. Howard-Bury later wrote about photographing the Head Lama: "After much persuasion, the other monks induced him to come outside and have his photograph taken, telling him he was an old man, and that his time on earth was short, and they would like to have a picture to remember him by."

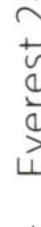

29

30

30. "Rongbuk Monastery and Mount Everest". Photographed and later hand-tinted by J. B. Noel, 1924 Mount Everest Expedition.

31

31. "At Rongbuk Monastery". All expedition members were blessed by the Head Lama, Dzatrul Rinpoche, before advancing up the mountain. Photographed by C. J. Morris for the 1922 Mount Everest Expedition.

JOHN CLAUDE WHITE

From the collections

Within the photographic collections of the Royal Geographical Society are 61 photographs taken by John Claude White (1853–1918). These combine to tell the story of White's work in Sikkim, Bhutan and Tibet at the turn of the century.

White was an engineer and photographer who in 1883 was assigned to the British Residency in Kathmandu, and who later served as Political Officer in Sikkim, which became a British Protectorate. As a consequence, he was also involved in British political relations in Tibet and Bhutan. This made White an obvious choice as one of Sir Francis Younghusband's deputies for the British Mission to Tibet in 1903–4.

White's photography represents the people and places of Sikkim, Bhutan and Tibet at a critical juncture in the history of the region. White was an amateur photographer working with glass plates and a large-format camera. His photographic work, taken on its own merit, is a striking political record of the times and those he encountered.

32. "Group of nuns at the nunnery of Taktsang", Tibet, 1904.

33. "Kampa Dzong". The fort built on top of an outcrop of rock was reached by a party reconnoitering during Sir Francis Younghusband's British Mission to Tibet, 1903–4.

34. Mr Claude White (standing), Sir Ugyen Wang Chuk (seated left), Major Rennick (seated centre) and Mr Paul (seated right), Bhutan, 1905.

35. "Paro Jong from the right bank of the Par Chhu", 1905.

36. "Tongsa Penlop's sister's family", Bhutan, 1905.

37. "The Abbot of Kampa Dzong", Tibet, 1904.

32

33

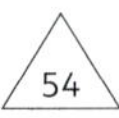

34

35

36

37

3

EARLY EXPEDITIONS

It took another 50 years following Radhanath Sikdar's calculation of the height of Peak XV (see "Mapping the Mountain", page 22) and Andrew Waugh's subsequent announcement to the Royal Geographical Society (RGS), naming Everest as the world's loftiest peak, before an organized Western expedition was sent to Everest with the aim of climbing the world's highest mountain. The mountain was simply too inaccessible and European mountaineering still largely centred on the Alps with occasional forays into other locations.

With both the North and South Poles reached in the early part of the twentieth century, all eyes had turned to the so-called "Third Pole": Everest. Having lost the race to both Poles, the British were keen to claim the third. During discussions at the RGS in 1919, Sir Francis Younghusband spoke of his determination that the first on the mountain "shall be a British expedition" and he hoped that it would be an "Englishman, or at any rate a Scotchman [sic], who would first climb Mount Everest". Only time and good fortune would tell if this dream would become a reality.

Western access to the mountain was still reliant on Tibetan goodwill. In 1921 the British were fortunate to receive their support for a reconnaissance expedition, with a notice issued by the Tibetan authorities requesting that Tibetans provide the expedition with all support necessary to approach the mountain (image 40, page 62). And approach they did. In 1921 the Mount Everest Reconnaissance Expedition, supported by porters, guides and climbers, was able to trek to and photograph Mount Everest and its approaches in great detail, as can be seen from the amazing shots taken by George Mallory and Charles Kenneth Howard-Bury (images 38, opposite, and 39, pages 60–61). The expertise and support that Indigenous Himalayans provided is in great evidence in the visual records from these expeditions, such as the roped-up porters in Howard Somervell's wonderful photograph (image 50, page 73). These photographs document the invaluable contribution of Indigenous peoples.

"It stands to reason that men with any zest for mountaineering could not possibly allow Mount Everest to remain untouched. The time, the opportunity, the money, the ability to make the necessary preliminary preparation might be lacking, but the wish and the will to stand on the summit of the world's highest mountain must have been in the heart of many a mountaineer since the Alps have been so firmly trampled underfoot."

– Sir Francis Younghusband, President of the Royal Geographical Society (1919–1922) and first Chairman of the Mount Everest Committe, Introduction to *Mount Everest: The Reconnaissance, 1921* (published 1922)

38. "Camp at 20,000 feet – The last day". Photographed by George Mallory during the 1921 Mount Everest Reconnaissance Expedition.

AN INACCESSIBLE MOUNTAIN

Essay by Eugene Rae

The beginning of a serious British attempt to climb Mount Everest can be said to date to 1905 when Lord Curzon, Viceroy of India, contacted Douglas Freshfield, who at different times was President of both the Alpine Club and the Royal Geographical Society (RGS), with the offer of £3,000 from the British Government of India towards the cost of mounting an expedition to either Everest or Kangchenjunga. Freshfield contacted the Alpine Club and began initiating an expedition, and then the RGS was brought on board. Things looked favourable, but approval was needed from the Secretary of State for India, John Morley. Unfortunately, Morley vetoed the expedition and that, for the time being, put an end to the schemes of the would-be conquerors of the mighty mountain.

With Tibet and Nepal closed to Europeans in the early years of the twentieth century, British climbers with an eye to the Himalayas had to content themselves with the peaks that lay within India. In 1907 Tom Longstaff led an expedition which made the first ascent of Trisul. This lofty peak has an altitude of 23,359ft (7,120m) and in climbing it Longstaff and his team were the first to ascend a mountain of over 22,965ft (7,000m). Four years later, in 1911, Alexander Kellas reached the summit of Pauhunri. At 23,386ft (7,128m), this remained the highest mountain climbed until 1930.

39

Even as climbers were tackling the mountains of northern India, efforts continued to persuade the India Office to sanction an approach to the Tibetan authorities regarding an expedition to Everest, and adventurers such as John Noel made illicit forays into Tibetan territory. The First World War put a temporary halt to the scheming, but with the cessation of hostilities, attempts to organize an expedition began anew. In 1920 Sir Francis Younghusband tried a different approach. He asked Charles Howard-Bury, an aristocratic soldier with impeccable connections, to persuade Sir Charles Bell, the British Political Officer for Bhutan, Sikkim and Tibet, to use his influence with the Tibetan authorities to negotiate permission for a passage through Tibet to Mount Everest. He was successful and permission was granted for the British to proceed in the following year, 1921. With that, the India Office withdrew its objections to the expedition and the project was officially approved.

A joint committee to co-ordinate and finance a reconnaissance expedition, formed of senior members of the Alpine Club and the RGS, was quickly set up. It was named the Mount Everest Committee (MEC). In recognition of his assistance in getting permission for the expedition, leadership was bestowed upon Charles Howard-Bury.

39. "The view from Windy Col Camp, at 22,500 ft., looking west and showing Everest, North Col and North Peak". This remarkable panoramic photograph was taken by C. K. Howard-Bury during the Mount Everest Reconnaissance Expedition of 1921.

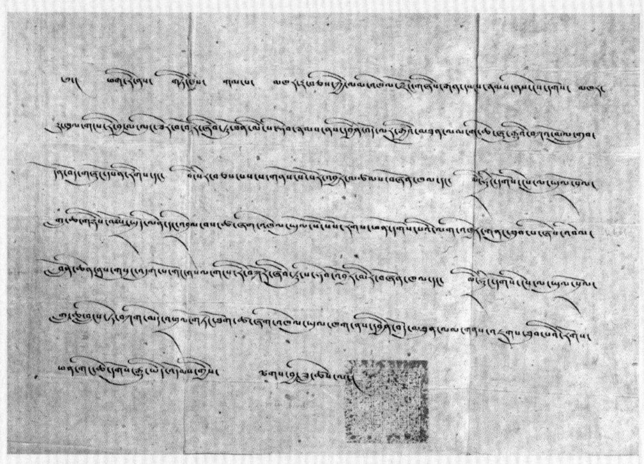

40

As news spread, men from all over the world attempted to join the expedition, but the MEC applied strict criteria that reflected the attitudes of the time. White British and Commonwealth men, drawn from the membership of the Alpine Club, would dominate the British mountaineering scene until after the Second World War. Women were not even considered.

The climbers chosen for the expedition were Harold Raeburn, a 56-year-old veteran of the Cairngorms and Alps; Alexander Kellas, who at 52 had already climbed higher than any other European climber; George Mallory, considered the best climber of his generation; and Henry Bullock, a friend of Mallory who replaced George Finch, originally picked but later rejected on medical grounds. The surveying team, from the Survey of India, consisted of Henry Morshead, Edward O. Wheeler, Lalbir Singh Thapa and Gujjar Singh. Also included were the expedition doctor and ornithologist, Sandy Wollaston, and geological surveyor, Alexander Heron.

The expedition members rendezvoused in Darjeeling where they engaged the services of a young Tibetan schoolmaster named Karma Paul. Paul was fluent in many languages, including Tibetan, Nepali and English, and served as the translator for this and future British expeditions. He also assisted with the recruitment of the expedition porters, including Sherpas for the high-altitude porterage. In mid-May they set off on the 300-mile march to Everest, mapping as they went. Towards the end of May, Kellas was taken ill and died as the expedition approached the Tibetan village of Kampa Dzong, from where the expedition members would have had their first sight of Everest. Four weeks after Kellas's death the expedition reached the Rongbuk Monastery and began to look for a way to approach the mountain.

In early August, Wheeler reached the head of the East Rongbuk Glacier, where he first sighted the North Col; further investigation suggested it might be the key to climbing Everest. On 21 September Bullock and Mallory made the first ascent of the Col, reaching 23,000ft (7,010m) before turning back due to a lack of equipment and supplies. Nevertheless, a way to the summit had been found. With the success of the reconnaissance expedition, the MEC launched a second expedition in 1922. This was a better equipped expedition which, it was hoped, would be able to reach the summit. It was led by Charles Granville Bruce, an officer in the Gurkha Rifles who placed great value on the role of Indigenous climbers, and included George Mallory; Tom Longstaff; Howard Somervell, a surgeon and amateur artist; Edward Norton, a career soldier and experienced climber; Geoffrey Bruce, cousin of Charles; and John Noel, who was to create a photographic record of the expedition.

40. The Prime Minister of Tibet's order to the Dzongpens and Headmen of Phari, Tinki, Kampa and Kharta, Iron Bird year (1921), asking them to give assistance to the British in getting to Everest.

41. George Finch's medical report on 17 March 1921, the results of which caused the offer of a place on the expedition to be withdrawn. It has been suggested that the medical report was falsified in order to prevent Finch, an Australian, taking part in the British expedition.

Also included on this 1922 expedition was George Finch. After being excluded from the 1921 expedition Finch had been involved in experiments in a decompression chamber at Oxford which had shown that the climbers would be unlikely to reach the summit of Everest without supplementary oxygen. On the strength of this, Finch had helped to develop the first practical oxygen set for high-altitude climbing and was determined to prove its worth. But not many of the other climbers shared his enthusiasm for this innovation.

The first attempt on the summit was made on 21 May 1922, by Norton, Somervell and Mallory, without supplementary oxygen. They reached 26,985ft (8,225m) and became the first to climb higher than 26,246ft (8,000m). On returning to Base Camp they were severely dehydrated; Somervell drank 17 cups of tea (3 litres) before he felt better.

It was now time for George Finch to test out the oxygen sets, which had been carried all the way from Darjeeling. Using supplementary oxygen and aided by Sherpa porters, Finch and Geoffrey Bruce, along with a young Gurkha soldier named Lans-Naik Tejbir Bura, established a new Camp V, another 500ft (150m) higher than Mallory, Norton and Somervell's climb. A storm forced them to spend the night and the following day sheltering in their tent before Finch, Bruce and Tejbir Bura set off for the summit again. Tejbir Bura, carrying a greater weight than the other two climbers, was forced to turn back due to exhaustion, but Bruce and Finch went on and reached 27,300ft (8,321m) before a fault with Bruce's oxygen set forced them to turn back.

Both the first and second attempts had been relatively successful, although the second arguably more so, as the efficacy of supplementary oxygen had been confirmed. A third attempt by Mallory, Somervell and Colin Crawford ended disastrously when seven porters, Lhakpa, Narbu, Pasang, Pemba, Sange, Temba and Antarge, were killed in an avalanche. The deaths provided a sombre end to the 1922 expedition.

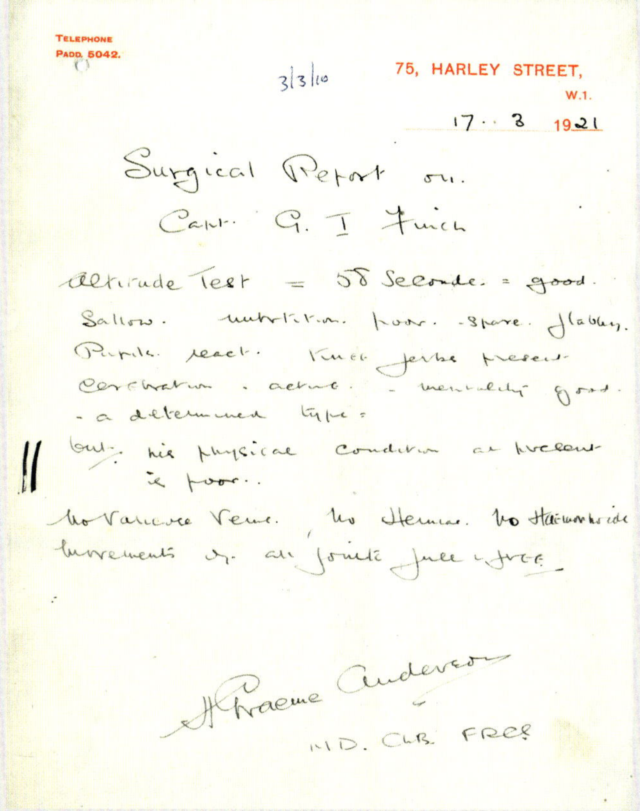

TELEPHONE
PADD. 5042.

3/3/10

75, HARLEY STREET,
W.1.

17 . 3 1921

Surgical Report on.
Capt. G. I Finch

Altitude Test = 58 Seconds = good.
Sallow. nutrition poor. spare. flabby.
Pupils react. Knee jerks present.
Cerebration. active. mentality good.
a determined type =
but: his physical condition at present is poor..
No Varicose Veins. No Hernia. No Haemorrhoids
Movements of all joints full & free

H Graeme Anderson
MD. ChB. FRCS

41

42

43

42. Members of the 1921 Mount Everest Reconnaissance Expedition in their camp, at 17,300ft (5,273m). Back row (left to right): Guy Bullock, Henry Morshead, Edward O. Wheeler and George Mallory. Front row (left to right): Alexander Heron, "Sandy" Wollaston, Charles Howard-Bury and Harold Raeburn. This photo has been credited to A. F. R. Wollaston but was likely taken by a porter.

43. "Temple at Lapchi Kang". Photographed by A. F. R. Wollaston during the 1921 Mount Everest Reconnaissance Expedition.

44

44. "Loading up at Dochen, below Chomolhari". A settlement at 14,700 ft (4,481m), to the north of Chomolhari (seen on the horizon), Dochen was one of the many Tibetan villages the expedition passed through on its route to Mount Everest. Photographed by C. K. Howard-Bury, 1921 Mount Everest Reconnaissance Expedition.

45. "Monks and Administrator at Shekar Chote". Photographed by C. K. Howard-Bury, 1921 Mount Everest Reconnaissance Expedition.

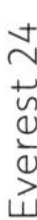

45

47

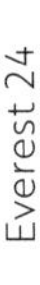

46. Pages 68–69: "Mount Everest, showing the South Peak, North Peak and North Col, from a peak 20,500ft above Advanced Camp". Photographed by G. L. Mallory during the 1921 Mount Everest Reconnaissance Expedition.

47. Members of the 1922 Mount Everest Expedition, including George Mallory and Sherpas, resting during the ascent of the North Col. Photographed by J. B. Noel.

48. In 1922, George Mallory and Edward Norton approached their record-setting height of 26,985ft (8,225m) on the Northeast Ridge of Mount Everest. Photographed by T. H. Somervell.

48

49. "The Second Climbing Party descending from their record climb". The photograph shows George Finch and Geoffrey Bruce as they head back to Camp IV at approximately 23,000ft (7,010m) on 27 May 1922. Finch and Bruce were accompanied for the majority of the climb by Gurkha NCO Lans-Naik Tejbir Bura. Photographed by A. Wakefield for the 1922 Mount Everest Expedition.

50. At the foot of the North Col, 1922 Mount Everest Expedition. On the expedition's third summit attempt on 7 June 1922 the climbing party triggered an avalanche, tragically killing seven Sherpas and ending the expedition. Photographed by T. H. Somervell.

49

50

ALEXANDER KELLAS

From the collections

The chemist and mountaineer Alexander Mitchell Kellas (1868–1921), regarded as "one of the great pioneers of Himalayan climbing", made his first expedition to the Himalayas in 1907, climbing in the Pir Panjal Range. He then made a remarkable series of climbs between 1909 and 1914, achieving the first ascents of Pauhunri (23,386ft/7,128m), Chomo Yummo (22,405ft/6,829m), Kangchengyao (22,602ft/6,889m) and several lesser peaks above 20,000ft (6,096m). His ascent of Pauhunri, with two Sherpas named Sona and Tuny, broke the existing summit altitude record. But this was not realized at the time due to an under-estimation of the mountain's height until the late twentieth century.

Kellas preferred to climb with just a few Sherpas by his side. He is credited with being the first European climber to recognize the crucial role and contributions of the Sherpas in supporting Himalayan expeditions. He is also renowned for his research into altitude and mountain sickness. While lecturer in Chemistry at the Middlesex Hospital Medical School (1900–19) he carried out extensive laboratory work on the effects of altitude on the human body, and in May 1916 Kellas read a paper at the Royal Geographical Society titled "A Consideration of the Possibility of Ascending the Loftier Himalaya", which addressed the physical problems of approaching Mount Everest and the physiological difficulties of climbing at high altitude. This research, combined with his Himalayan climbing experience and knowledge of the abilities of the Sherpas, was unrivalled. For this reason, Kellas was invited to join the 1921 Mount Everest Reconnaissance Expedition. Tragically, at the age of 56, he suffered a fatal heart attack on the expedition's approach to Kampa Dzong.

The RGS holds over 500 of Kellas's photographs, representing some of the earliest photographs of the Himalayan mountains.

51

"I, who knew Kellas well, believe that if he had not died, Everest would have been conquered by now, and by nothing other than this – the combination of Kellas's Himalayan knowledge and Mallory's dash."

– John Noel, *Through Tibet to Everest*, 1927

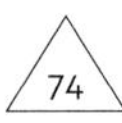

51. Tibetan Sherpas roped up on snow, Sikkim, 1907. It was the work of Alexander Kellas, at the turn of the century, that brought the value of Sherpas to the attention of the British climbing fraternity.

52. Sherpa porters on a pass in Sikkim.

53. Climbers in an ice field.

54. "View to the south from the summit of Pawhunri". It is assumed that the two Sherpa porters to the right of the photograph are Tuny and Sona.

52

53

54

4

INDIGENOUS INTERMEDIARIES

The work of Indigenous Himalayans was hugely important to the success of the 1924 Mount Everest Expedition, their value having been demonstrated by the 1921 and 1922 expeditions. The British depended heavily on their physical labour, skills and local knowledge not only to transport provisions, negotiate with local authorities, and assist on climbs at the higher altitudes, but also to safely navigate the expedition members through the unfamiliar environments.

British attitudes towards porters and other Indigenous intermediaries reflected the cultural attitudes of the times, but some were quick to realize their worth. Alexander Kellas recognized the ability of Sherpas at high altitudes during his earliest Himalayan climbs and championed them as porters on future Everest expeditions. And in his account of the 1924 expedition, *The Fight for Everest: 1924*, Edward Norton wrote that the high-altitude porters were "a splendid bodyof men, on whose shoulders we literally climbed Mount Everest".

Overall, however, a recognition of the invaluable work of all Indigenous participants on the expedition was limited, and they were often regarded by the British climbers as inferior members of the team. This attitude was increasingly challenged through the 1920s and 1930s by some European climbers and the Sherpas themselves. By the expeditions of the 1950s Sherpas such as Tenzing Norgay were increasingly being regarded as equal climbing partners.

This chapter highlights the sheer number of Tibetans and Sherpas whose expertise was required for each expedition. Some were repeatedly involved in many of the Everest parties over the years and regarded as indispensable, including Karma Paul, who can be seen in photographs of the 1922 and 1936 expeditions (images 56, 61, 65 and 66). The images featured in this chapter also reveal the many different roles that the Indigenous intermediaries fulfilled, whether as high-altitude "Tigers", photographic porters, shoemakers or interpreters.

"If you can teach these soldiers to act as good mountain guides, then you have solved the problem of the snowy Himalayas."

– Douglas Freshfield, President of the Royal Geographical Society (1914–1917), "Exploration in the Mustagh Mountains: Discussion", *The Geographical Journal*, October 1893

55. A group of porters on the North Col. Photographed by J. B. Noel during the 1922 Mount Everest Expedition.

55

CROSSING CULTURES: INTERPRETERS AND OTHER INTERMEDIARIES

Essay by Professor Felix Driver

There is a pivotal scene in John Noel's 1922 film *Climbing Mount Everest* in which the interpreter Karma Paul is shown introducing the climbers and porters, one by one, to the Head Lama of the Rongbuk Monastery in order to receive his blessing. Dressed in Western attire and fluent in both Tibetan and English, Paul is shown performing the role of diplomatic go-between, as he passes from the covered dais housing the lamas to the courtyard where the climbers and porters are seated. Presented as a crucial moment of authorization for the attempted ascent of Everest, the scene was actually filmed on the way down from the mountain, following an avalanche that had killed seven porters on 7 June. Nothing is recorded of Karma Paul's response to this disaster, although his command of Himalayan languages would surely have allowed him closer insights into the impact on the surviving porters than those available to the British climbers.

Karma Paul was a Tibetan of modest means, born in Lhasa but raised as an orphan from the age of eight by missionaries in Darjeeling, where he began his working life as a teacher, taxi driver and clerk. His subsequent employment on all the British expeditions to Mount Everest from 1922 to 1938 can be traced through the manuscript and photographic archives at the Royal Geographical Society (RGS). Initially his role was to act as interpreter in the expedition's negotiations with local authorities, including lamas and dzongpens (district governors), along the route to Everest. In later expeditions he came to act as a sirdar (overseer) of the porters, having a decisive influence on recruitment that continued until at least 1948, as Tenzing Norgay later recalled.

The role of interpretation, vital to all acts of diplomacy, confers on the translator a special status. In the case of the Everest expeditions, knowledge of Tibetan among the climbers was limited, and the sensitivities surrounding a British presence in Tibet required considerable tact in dealing with the local authorities. Karma Paul's linguistic skills extended beyond Tibetan to Nepali, Urdu, Bengali, Sikkimese and Lepcha. While the climbers eventually came to remember him fondly, a group of them later commissioning a portrait now in the RGS collection, Geoffrey Bruce patronizingly described him in 1924 as "a rather vain youth and apt to be a little carried away by his own abilities". His cross-cultural competence attracted suspicion as well as praise. As Bruce's cousin, Charles Granville Bruce, put it: "When he was Karma he was a Buddhist, and received blessings from every Lama he could get near to. When he was Paul he was a Christian."

Karma Paul was not the only interpreter employed on Everest expeditions during the 1920s. Others included Gyalzen Kazi and Chhetan Wangdi, who

56. "Karma Paul with the Dzongpen of Shekar". Karma Paul's interpretation skills and knowledge of Tibetan customs were vital in expedition negotiations with local governers. Photographed by C. J. Morris for the 1922 Mount Everest Expedition; later hand-tinted by J. B. Noel.

56

were interpreters for the 1921 Mount Everest Reconnaissance Expedition. Kazi was a member of a high-ranking Sikkimese family and also employed in 1922 and 1924; Wangdi had served in the Tibetan Army and for the Indian Army in Egypt during the First World War. They were valued highly by the expedition leader Charles Howard-Bury: "their tact and knowledge of Tibetan ways and customs were of the greatest use in keeping up the friendly relations established between the expedition and the Tibetans."

As Karma Paul's role expanded to include oversight of expedition porters in the 1930s, his ability to navigate the colonial world-view of the British and the cultural expectations of Himalayan porters became even more important. His status rose accordingly. In 1936, he was pictured outside the Planters' Club in Darjeeling deliberating with the leaders of the expedition of that year. He also features in an album sheet of photographic portraits

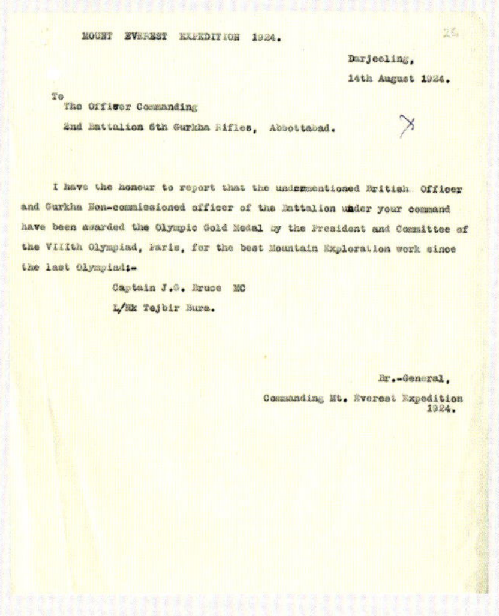

MOUNT EVEREST EXPEDITION 1924.

Darjeeling,
14th August 1924.

To
The Officer Commanding
2nd Battalion 6th Gurkha Rifles, Abbottabad.

I have the honour to report that the undermentioned British Officer and Gurkha Non-commissioned officer of the Battalion under your command have been awarded the Olympic Gold Medal by the President and Committee of the VIIIth Olympiad, Paris, for the best Mountain Exploration work since the last Olympiad:-

Captain J.G. Bruce MC
L/Nk Tejbir Bura.

Br.-General,
Commanding Mt. Everest Expedition 1924.

57

57. Letter from Geoffrey Bruce, August 1924, to "The Officer Commanding, 2nd Battalion 6th Gurkha Rifles" announcing the Olympic Gold Medal had been awarded to Tejbir Bura.

58. John Macdonald (back row, right) stands with other members of the 1924 Mount Everest Expedition team. Back row (left to right): Andrew Irvine, George Mallory, Edward Norton, Noel Odell and John Macdonald. Front row (left to right): Edward O. Shebbeare, Geoffrey Bruce, T. Howard Somervell and Bentley Beetham. Photographed by J. B. Noel.

by Jim Gavin (see image 152, page 182), along with dozens of Sherpas and other porters recruited for the expedition, each of whom were issued with identity tags. Like the British climbers, he needed no such identifier, although as a mark of distinction he proudly wore the robes of an elite Tibetan.

While interpreters are a special kind of intermediary, the experience of cross-cultural communication was shared by many others involved in the early Everest expeditions. Indigenous people could be found across the workforce, from porters to high-altitude climbers, although none matched the celebrity of Tenzing Norgay after his successful ascent in 1953. The Asian officers on the 1921 reconnaissance expedition included Gujjar Singh and Lalbir Singh Thapa and the photographer Abdul Jalil Khan, who worked on a comprehensive survey alongside British officers. In the 1922 and 1924 expeditions, Tibetans, Lepcha and other Indigenous Himalayans were employed as plant collectors, cooks, tailors and cobblers, the last a particularly vital role in protecting climbers' feet from frostbite. Most of their work went uncelebrated, with a few exceptions: some officers in the Gurkha regiment (such as the Nepalese Tejbir Bura) were awarded medals at the Winter Olympics in 1924, although this appears to have been an afterthought following awards made to the British climbers earlier in the year.

Intermediaries supporting Everest expeditions also included residents of dual heritage such as David Macdonald, the son of a Sikkimese Lepcha woman and a Scottish planter. Macdonald had attended the Bhotiya school in Darjeeling associated with the work of the pundits, such as Sarat Chandra Das, who mapped Tibet for the British. He served as an interpreter on the British military mission to Lhasa in 1904 and later became British Trade Agent in Yatung, Tibet. He was fluent in many regional languages and involved in the publication of Tibetan dictionaries, glossaries and guides for European travellers, later establishing the Himalayan Hotel in Kalimpong, a familiar destination for many travellers to Darjeeling. While Macdonald played a key role supporting the Everest expeditions through his close dealings with local authorities in Tibet, his son John joined the 1924 expedition party in Tibet, taking responsibility for communications. John Macdonald is pictured in some of the most iconic group portraits of the climbers on the 1924 expedition.

While some members of the early British expeditions to Tibet, notably Howard Somervell, tried hard to understand the peoples and cultures they encountered, their efforts were rudimentary at best. They relied heavily on intermediaries with knowledge of local languages for even the most basic of communications concerning provisioning and portering, and even more so for the diplomacy required within the borders of Tibet. This dependence was always tinged with suspicion and sometimes accompanied by explicit criticism of Tibetans like Karma Paul or Europeans of mixed heritage such as John Macdonald. Crossing between cultures can be just as challenging as climbing mountains.

58

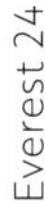

59

59. Gyalzen Kazi, from Gangtok in Sikkim, and Chhetan Wangdi, a Tibetan who had fought with the Indian Army in Egypt, were employed as interpreters on the 1921 Mount Everest Reconnaissance Expedition. Photographed by A. F. R. Wollaston.

60. Moti, one of the shoemakers for the 1922 Mount Everest Expedition. Photographed by J. B. Noel.

60

61

61. Karma Paul (behind the table) is seated alongside Charles Granville Bruce interviewing dzongpens (district governors) in Kampa Dzong. Photographed by J. B. Noel during the 1922 Mount Everest Expedition.

62. Photographer John Noel and his photographic porters, 1922. The photograph shows Noel with the team of eight men who carried his photographic equipment, supported by a mule and muleteer. They are pictured behind their equipment, including the Newman Sinclair camera, a tripod and telephoto lens. This image was previously credited to John Noel, but was likely taken by a porter.

62

63

64

63. A group of six high-altitude "Tigers" from the 1924 Mount Everest Expedition, who were accorded the highest status by the British climbers. Photographed by J. B. Noel.

64. Sherpa families' thumbprints proving receipt of payment on 1 May 1924 for work on the 1924 Mount Everest Expedition.

65

66

65. Karma Paul (left), the expedition's interpreter, issues identity discs which the porters wore around their necks. Photographer unknown, 1936 Mount Everest Expedition.

66. Karma Paul (left) with Jemadar Lachhman Singh Sahi, of the Gurkha Rifles, who assisted Percy Wynn-Harris with the accounts for the 1936 Mount Everest Expedition and was also responsible for the management of the glacier camps. Photographed by F. S. Smythe.

RECRUITMENT OF INDIGENOUS HIMALAYANS

From the collections

Prior to the arrival of the British climbers in Darjeeling in March 1924, a local agent named V. E. Weatherall was appointed to advertise the expedition and gather together a large number of Sherpas, Bhotiya and other Indigenous Himalayans keen to apply for work on the expedition. Once the British climbers had arrived, recruitment could begin for the varying roles, including cooks, porters, bootmakers, interpreters and high-altitude climbers. Those with previous expedition experience and who were considered to have perfomed well were automatically selected.

Recruitment in 1924 was based on the British climbers' experience of the porters during the previous two Mount Everest expeditions and used basic medical assessments and observations, such as chest size. For example, Edward Norton, who took over as leader of the 1924 expedition following Charles Granville Bruce's retirement due to ill health, referred to a preference for a man of "light and wiry" build and "a good-class man of some intelligence" for the high-altitude porters.

Further recruitment lines would be set up as the expedition continued to journey through Tibet. Between Shekar and Rongbuk, just over 150 Tibetans, including men, women and children, were recruited with permission from the Dzongpen of Shekar to transport the provisions from Base Camp to Camps I and II. Bruce later wrote of his astonishment at how one woman was able to carry her two-year-old child on top of the 18-kg (40-lb) load, the weight carried by each Tibetan, regardless of sex or age.

67

"We had, as usual, a very amusing time picking our personnel. There were several old followers... and among them turned up my former porter and henchman, Llakpa Chédé [sic], who in 1922 had done his best to come, but was as that time very ill with malaria... We took with us a larger outfit of porters than in 1922, but on the whole, an equally satisfactory lot."

– Charles Granville Bruce, *The Fight for Everest: 1924*

67. "Taking laborers' dependents thumbprints". The families of those employed on the expedition received monthly pay on behalf of the men. Photographed by J. B. Noel.

68. Recruitment of labourers, Darjeeling, for the 1924 Mount Everest Expedition. Photographed by N. E. Odell.

69. The local workforce of the 1924 Mount Everest Expedition, including Karma Paul (standing sixth from the right). Photographed by N. E. Odell.

70. "Loading up at Base Camp". Tibetans were expected to carry greater weights than the British climbers. Photographed by A. C. Irvine during the 1924 Mount Everest Expedition.

68

69

70

5

1924

The tragic end to the 1922 expedition did little to dampen the British enthusiasm for climbing Mount Everest and another expedition was organized for 1924. Leadership was again given to Charles Granville Bruce, but an attack of malaria at the start of the expedition caused him to withdraw and Edward Norton assumed the mantle. Also included were Geoffrey Bruce, Noel Odell, Howard Somervell, Edward Shebbeare, Richard Hingston, Bentley Beetham, John de Vars Hazard, George Mallory, Andrew Irvine and John Noel. The latter made a substantial donation to the expedition in exchange for sole rights to the cinematic and photographic output.

A notable absentee was George Finch, who, having proved the efficacy of oxygen both in climbing and at rest in 1922, did not even make the shortlist in 1924. Finch was not only an innovator but also a first-rate climber, and his omission was unfortunate. Nevertheless, a strong and experienced team had been selected with only Andrew Irvine lacking substantial mountaineering experience: it was hoped that his youth and strength would be suitable compensation. The Mount Everest Committee were confident that the planning and preparation for the 1924 Mount Everest Expedition would bring success.

The hand-coloured lantern slide by John Noel shown on the facing page (image 71) portrays the members of the 1924 team as relaxed and confident. There were early setbacks, however, with illness afflicting both the leader, Charles Bruce, and Bentley Beetham, who was prevented from climbing. Beetham's personal disappointment did bring the benefit of his exceptional photographic skills as he set about documenting the journey to Everest. His landscape photographs, such as image 75 (page 103), give a sense of the scale and drama of the mountain. Beetham's images add an extra dimension to John Noel's high-altitude photographs, such as his spectacular shot of Base Camp dwarfed by the Rongbuk Glacier and the North Face of Everest (image 78, page 106).

"...in short, no trouble has been spared to equip this Third Expedition after fullest consideration of the experiences of previous years, and the Committee feel confident that if only the weather is kind we shall learn this year the extreme of human possibility, which it may be predicted will not fall short of the summit."

– "The Mount Everest Expedition of 1924", *The Geographical Journal*, 1924

71. Members of the 1924 British Mount Everest expedition. Back row (left to right): Andrew Irvine, George Mallory, Edward Norton, Noel Odell and John Macdonald. Front row (left to right): Edward O. Shebbeare, Geoffrey Bruce, T. Howard Somervell and Bentley Beetham. Hand-tinted photograph by J. B. Noel.

71

RETURN TO TIBET

Essay by Eugene Rae

Although he was one of the first selected for the 1924 expedition, George Mallory expressed some misgivings about returning to the mountain. At this point, he was working as a lecturer with the Cambridge University Extramural Studies Department and to join the expedition he would have to obtain leave from the University. He was also concerned about leaving his wife Ruth and three young children again; out of the past three years more than 12 months had been spent on expedition. Mallory was also unhappy to discover that George Finch was not to be offered a place. However, the pull of the mountain was strong and with the intervention of various people, including Arthur Hinks who wrote to the University to explain the necessity of Mallory taking part in the expedition, Mallory's doubts were allayed. In November 1923 he wrote to Hinks:

> *Just a line to let you know that I'm now quite determined to go out again. Rather a try altogether, but I'm very happy now it is decided. The doctors think me A1... Many thanks for your good offices in the matter.*

At 22, the youngest member of the expedition was Andrew Irvine, a champion rower, who helped Oxford to victory in the Boat Race in 1924, and a gifted engineer. Irvine had recently returned from an expedition to Spitsbergen, where he had impressed one companion, Tom Longstaff, who, as it happened, sat on the selection panel for the 1924 Mount Everest Expedition. Irvine had also made a favourable impression on Noel Odell when, in the summer of 1919, Odell and his wife had met him on the summit of a Welsh mountain. Not content with hiking up the trail, Irvine had ridden his motorcycle to the top. Irvine's engineering ability also went in his favour, and along with Odell he was assigned the responsibility of looking after the supplementary oxygen. Shortly before setting off, Irvine wrote to Sydney Spencer, Joint Secretary of the Mount Everest Committee:

> *I enclose herewith the list of tools I should suggest, to make a small tool-kit for looking after the oxygen apparatus...they will all pack in quite a small box and none are very heavy...*

With all the personnel selected and the equipment and supplies in place, those members of the team not already in India made their way to Mumbai by ship. Mallory, Irvine, Bentley Beetham and John de Vars Hazard travelled by the SS *California* from Liverpool. From Mumbai they went by rail to Kolkata and then on to Darjeeling where they again retained the services of Karma Paul and his assistant Gyalzen Kazi. Also assigned were Moti the cobbler and Rhombu the naturalist, both of whom had taken part in the 1922 expedition. Four Gurkha non-commissioned officers were also

72

seconded to the expedition. Several hundred pack animals were hired to carry the equipment and supplies into Tibet and Himalayan porters, mainly Sherpas, were recruited to carry everything needed for the summit attempts from Base Camp up to the higher camps.

The party departed Darjeeling on the 25 March, heading north and rapidly gaining altitude as they went. Crossing the Jelep La (Pass) at 14,390ft (4,386m), they arrived in Tibet and followed the Chumbi Valley to the town of Phari. They were now on the Tibetan Plateau and, turning west, they followed the route familiar from the previous expeditions, stopping at towns such as Kampa Dzong, Tingri and Shekar Dzong along the way. The journey was punctuated by bouts of illness caused by the cold wind, dust and insanitary conditions they encountered on the plateau and by practice climbs to help with acclimatization.

72. "Everest team members loading horses at Sedongchen". Photographed by B. Beetham.

73. "Everest from Pang La", 1924. Andrew Irvine (right), George Mallory (to Irvine's left) and two unknown porters rest at the top of the Pang La Pass to admire the snowy peaks of Everest and the wider Himalayan mountain range. Photographed by N. E. Odell.

73

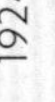
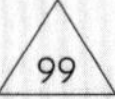

74. "Rongbuk Monastery with Everest in the distance". Base Camp was established four miles up the valley from the monastery, on the same site as the previous two expeditions. Norton later wrote how the old camping ground "looked as if we had only left it yesterday". Photographed by B. Beetham.

They arrived at Rongbuk Monastery at the end of April and shortly after established Base Camp at 16,800ft (5,120m). Edward Norton wrote:

> *So finished the first phase of the Expedition; we were up to time, and we had a surprisingly clean bill of health. So smoothly had the machine run so far that we may be pardoned if we were optimistic as to the future.*

Norton's optimism seemed well placed as, on 30 April, they began the next stage of the expedition: establishing three camps on the East Rongbuk Glacier and a camp on the North Col (Camp IV). Additional porters had been recruited in Tibet especially for this phase and, supervised by the Gurkha NCOs, Camps I and II were provisioned without any serious issue. Camp III was to prove a much harder proposition and on 11 May, after several days of severe cold and ferocious winds, Norton decided on a general retreat, and climbers and porters alike returned to Base Camp to recuperate.

On the way down, Man Bahadur, one of the cobblers, died of pneumonia following severe frostbite in both feet, and Lance-Naik Shamsherpun, one of the Gurkhas, suffered a brain haemorrhage. Only major surgery could have saved them, and tragically they both died and were buried in a sheltered spot near to Base Camp. Following the loss of Shamsherpun, Norton wrote: "By his death the expedition were the poorer of a gallant and loyal young man, who had worked with the most conspicuous and whole-hearted zeal throughout."

After a few days of rest at Base Camp the remaining climbers and porters were fit enough to attend a blessing ceremony at Rongbuk Monastery. Soon after, the weather improved sufficiently for the reoccupation of the glacier camps and by the end of 19 May, Camp III was fully occupied and the challenging task of provisioning Camp IV began.

74

1924

75. "Near Kupup – ascending Jelep La".
A British expedition member travels on a mule accompanied by a porter on foot. Photographed by B. Beetham.

75

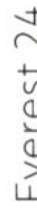

76

77

76. "A group at the Dzongpen's Shekar", including George Mallory (third from left), Edward Norton (fourth from left), the Dzongpen of Shekar (second from right) and Geoffrey Bruce (far right). Photographed by J. B. Noel.

77. "After blessing ceremony by Holy Lama, Rongbuk". Due to the Head Lama's illness, it was not until after the expedition was forced to retreat to Base Camp due to bad weather that they received the blessing from Dzatrul Rinpoche. Photographed by N. E. Odell.

78

78. "The north face of Everest and Rongbuk Glacier (showing glacial moraine) and Base Camp". The tiny tents of Base Camp are dwarfed by the scale of Mount Everest and the surrounding peaks. Photographed by B. Beetham.

79. An expedition member explores the ice pinnacles of East Rongbuk Glacier. This photograph is looking north towards Kellas Rock Peak and shows a frozen lake where the expedition rested for half an hour on their trek through the glacier. Photographed by J. B. Noel.

79

80. Pages from the Camp III diary, 5 May to 11 June 1924. Camp diaries were used to record weather conditions, food and store logs and to track expedition members' movements between camps. One entry from 11 May, written by Howard Somervell, writes of "the hardest day I have ever seen anywhere. Wind, snow, no sun to speak of, almost impossible to live outside".

80

81. "Great crevasses in the glacier". An expedition member examines a steep crevasse as the party moves up the East Rongbuk Glacier. Photographed by J. B. Noel.

81

82

82. This photograph shows the first party ascending the "Trough" in the East Rongbuk Glacier, towards Camp III. The second party can be seen in the distance, dwarfed by the glacier. They reached Camp III at 6pm on 5 May. Photographed by A. C. Irvine.

SUPPLEMENTARY OXYGEN

From the collections

The first recorded use of supplementary oxygen in the Himalayas was in 1907 during Tom Longstaff's ascent of Trisul. However, little was noted of its use and effectiveness. A decade later, Alexander Kellas presented a paper to the Society titled "A Consideration of the Possibility of Ascending the Loftier Himalaya", which discussed the physiological and physical challenges of climbing the highest Himalayan peaks. Kellas's research into the physiological effects of high-altitude balloon ascents revealed that oxygen was immensely helpful at high altitudes and his experiments with supplementary oxygen during his ascent of Kamet in 1920 helped to inform the planning of the 1921 Mount Everest Reconnaissance Expedition. Bottled oxygen was taken on the expedition but due to Kellas's death on the approach to Mount Everest the oxygen was never used.

Supplementary oxygen was again considered for the 1922 Mount Everest Expedition, largely due to the efforts of the Australian physical chemist George Finch, who had conducted experiments in a high-altitude chamber in Oxford with Georges Dreyer and P. J. H. Unna. Finch had initially been invited to join the 1921 expedition before a second medical examination ruled him unfit. The "English air", as it was called by the porters, proved to be a great success in 1922 when Geoffrey Bruce and Finch set a new altitude record of 27,300ft (8,321m), clearly demonstrating an advantage over the climbers without the aid of oxygen. However, the use of supplementary oxygen was a matter of debate for the climbing community in the 1920s with some believing it to be artificial and unsporting. Finch was a firm believer in its use.

The 1924 expedition's apparatus was based on Finch's modified version of the 1922 apparatus and included a lighter cylinder with increased capacity. Remarkably, Finch was not invited to join the 1924 expedition or any future Everest expeditions, but his pioneering oxygen work would prove invaluable for a successful summit.

83

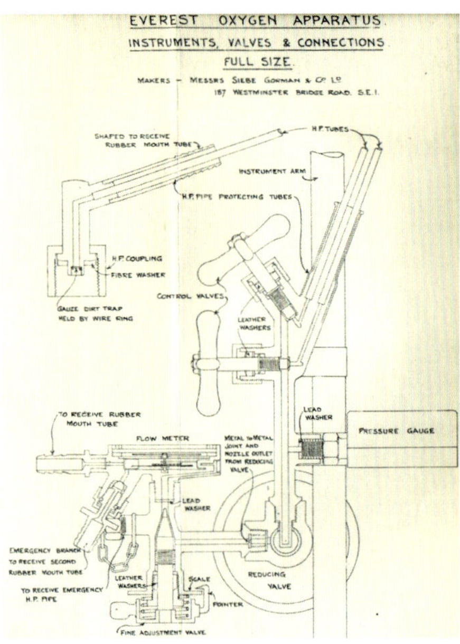

84

85

"I would remind the accuser that, by the inhalation of a little life-giving gas, the climber does not smooth away the rough rocks of the mountain or still the storm; nor is he an Aladdin who, by a rub on a magic ring, is wafted by invisible agents to his goal. Oxygen renders available more of his store of energy and so hastens his steps, but it does not, alas! Fit the wings of Mercury on his feet. The logic of the anti-oxygenist is surely faulty."

– George Finch, *The Geographical Journal*, December 1922

86

87

83. A four-cylinder oxygen set used on the 1922 Mount Everest Expedition and which belonged to George Finch.

84. Diagram of the 1924 Mount Everest Expedition oxygen apparatus, showing the instruments, valves and connections.

85. George Finch, seen here wearing the oxygen apparatus for the 1922 expedition, worked tirelessly to improve the system and made modifications to the apparatus for the 1924 expedition. Photographed, then hand-tinted, by J. B. Noel.

86. "Captain Finch and oxygen equipment", 1922 Mount Everest Expedition. Finch believed strongly in the use of oxygen equipment to aid climbing. Photographed by J. B. Noel.

87. "Irvine with oxygen cylinders". Andrew Irvine shared responsibility for the oxygen apparatus with Noel Odell on the 1924 Mount Everest Expedition. Photographed by B. Beetham.

6

THE FINAL APPROACH

With Camp III reoccupied and an improvement in the weather conditions, the expedition's next challenge was to find a safe route up to the North Col – a "dangerous wall of ice, like a trap set at the foot of the mountain", as Geoffrey Bruce later wrote – and establish Camp IV. George Mallory and Edward Norton led the way with Noel Odell and Lhakpa Tsering, described by Norton as "a wiry and active porter", in support. They were followed by relays of Sherpa porters.

The new route to the North Col, avoiding the avalanche risk areas of the route taken in 1922, required a good deal of hard climbing, including ascending a 200ft (60m) iced-up chimney (the mountaineering term for a vertical crack large enough to climb inside). The porters could not climb the chimney burdened with their packs, so the heavy loads had to be hauled up by rope, a task at which Andrew Irvine excelled. Camp IV was successfully established on 21 May. However, the expedition's struggles to establish the camp had weakened the party.

Frustratingly, the weather conditions again deteriorated, and the climbers were forced to retreat for the second time. At Camp I, a "council of war" was held for the party to regroup and put together a plan for another attempt at establishing the higher camps. For this work, 15 of the fittest and strongest Sherpa porters were chosen. Nicknamed the "Tigers", these men included Norbu Yishe, Lhakpa Chjedi, Semchumbi, Dorjay Pasang and Lobsang Tashi. With the monsoon looming, a plan was also made for an attempt on the summit at the earliest possible opportunity: Mallory and Bruce were to make the first attempt, Norton and Howard Somervell the second, with Odell and Irvine in support for both at Camp IV. The climbers had now reached the point where their plans and dreams could be fulfilled.

The 1924 team included a number of accomplished photographers, among them Bentley Beetham, who took the daunting shot "Climbing the North Col" (image 93, page 122). They also included the professional photographer and cinematographer John Noel, who had paid £8,000 for the photographic rights, a crucial sum in enabling the expedition to go ahead. The most dramatic sequence was obtained by Howard Somervell during his summit attempt with Edward Norton, recording their progress to a new height record of just over 28,000ft. Somervell's final shot marked the highest point on earth at which anyone had taken photographs.

"Progress up the north ridge of Everest does not lend itself to description. It is a fight against the wind and altitude, generally on rock, sometimes on snow, at an average angle of 45°."

– Edward Norton, *The Fight for Everest: 1924*

88. "The north face and summit of Mount Everest." Bentley Beetham took this photograph as he approached Camp III below the North Col. At the centre is the great gully or couloir which Edward Norton crossed on his summit attempt. The summit rises to the right of the frame beyond.

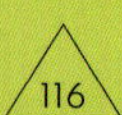

THE NORTH FACE

Essay by Peter Gillman

At 6am on 1 June, George Mallory and Geoffrey Bruce, supported by eight high-altitude Sherpa porters, left the North Col on the 1924 expedition's first summit attempt. Although the day had dawned fair, when they crested the broad North Ridge above the North Col they were hit by a bitter northeasterly wind. Mallory had hoped to site what would be Camp V at 25,300ft (7,711m), but they were still 300ft (91m) short when four of the porters said they could go no further. The others pushed on, finally pitching two tiny tents at 25,200ft (7,681m) on crumbling rock on the lee side of the ridge. Five of the porters returned to the North Col, leaving three to carry loads the next day. But the morning brought disappointment when the porters said they were too tired to carry on. "Apparently the wind had taken the heart out of them," Edward Norton wrote. Mallory had hoped to position the next camp at 27,000ft (8,230m) – 2,000ft (610m) below the summit – but with no porters to assist them, they were compelled to return to the North Col.

On that same day, 2 June, Norton and Howard Somervell set off from the North Col with six porters on their own summit attempt. Some two hours out, they were surprised to see Mallory and Bruce, plus their porters, descending towards them – "a grievous disappointment", Somervell commented. He and Norton stopped at Mallory's Camp V that night and the next day, 3 June, reached 26,800ft (8,169m), scraping out a ledge to pitch the tent that comprised Camp VI, while their three remaining porters descended to the North Col. They left camp at 6.40am the next day, 4 June, deciding to aim for the Great Couloir bisecting the face and, once across it, strike up to the final summit pyramid. After an hour they reached the Yellow Band, the vast stratum of sandstone that crosses the North Face, finding that it consisted of a series of sloping slabs and ledges that gave only insecure footholds. As the altitude took its toll, their progress slowed, and it was midday when they neared the Great Couloir. Somervell was at the limit of his strength, with a parched throat and a hacking cough. He sat down on a boulder and told Norton to go on alone.

Norton continued for another hour. The couloir was full of waist-deep snow and the rock beyond was even steeper. He now made the disastrous mistake of removing his goggles, suspecting they were impairing his sight, but this was most likely due to oxygen starvation. At 1pm, half-blind, he halted. The summit was still some 800–900ft (244–274m) higher, so he turned back. When Norton reached Somervell they embarked on their descent – "with almost a feeling of relief that our worst trials were over", Somervell wrote. They were not. They had reached 25,000ft (7,620m) and dusk was falling when Somervell succumbed to a renewed bout of coughing. Something lodged in his throat and he began choking to death. While Norton walked on unaware, Somervell pummelled his chest, coughing up the obstruction – part of the mucous membrane of his larynx that had been damaged by frostbite. After spitting it out, along with some blood, he could breathe again.

The two men continued down, signalling with a torch as they neared the North Col. Mallory and Noel Odell climbed to meet them, escorting them to the Col where they plied them with tea and soup. Their companions, Norton wrote, "were kindness itself" and congratulated them on establishing a new height record – "though we ourselves felt nothing but disappointment at our failure."

On the evening of 4 June, Norton crawled into his sleeping bag in his tent on the North Col. Virtually blind and in intense pain, he sensed that Mallory had climbed into his sleeping bag alongside him. Then Mallory announced that he wanted to make one more summit attempt. "I entirely agreed with his decision," Norton wrote, "and was full of admiration for the indomitable spirit of the man."

For Mallory, the decision appeared compelling. He was the only man who had been on all three expeditions – 1921, 1922 and 1924. He had pioneered the route, finding the North Col after months of searching in 1921 and going high in 1922. On each occasion he had left his wife Ruth and their three young children behind at home. Ruth, although loyal to a fault, had made her discomfort clear before they parted once more. Mallory had as good as promised this would be his last attempt – and dreamed of a new life and career if he succeeded.

So, what of his chances? From this distance, there appear to be three factors to consider: clothing and equipment; supplementary oxygen; and the choice of route. In respect of the first, it has sometimes been fashionable to cast the early Everest climbers as innocents abroad, ignorant of the odds they faced. George Bernard Shaw commented that in a group photograph the climbers looked as if they were at a "Connemara picnic surprised by a snowstorm". Some of the climbers photographed in 1921 were indeed wearing Norfolk jackets, knickerbockers, puttees (lower leg coverings) and trilbies. But these were typically worn for the long march across Tibet or life in Base Camp rather than high-altitude climbing. For that, the expedition was state of the art, benefitting from the experience of Polar exploration and research conducted to assist the pioneering First World War pilots. High-altitude climbers – Mallory

89

90

89. Edward Norton (1884–1954), photographed by J. B. Noel.

90. Dr T. Howard Somervell (1890–1975), photographed by B. Beetham.

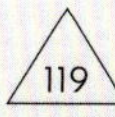

included – wore windproof cotton "Shackleton" jackets developed for the Antarctic and were equipped with fur-lined leather motorcycle helmets; for undergarments they wore alternate layers of cotton or wool and silk.

Mallory favoured some personal items, too: a flannel shirt from Paine's Outfitters in Godalming, Surrey, England; a brown, long-sleeved pullover; and a patterned waistcoat made by Ruth. He wore leather boots studded with V-shaped nails for grip. Compared to modern hi-tech gear, the 1924 clothing may appear primitive. But, given good weather, which was still holding over Everest in the fateful first week of June 1924, the clothing was not a decisive factor.

The use of oxygen equipment proved to be a more controversial matter. Mallory had never climbed with supplementary oxygen before, but now resolved to do so. It too was based on equipment developed for First World War pilots and was intended to compensate for the paucity of oxygen at high altitude. Some climbers regarded using oxygen as an unfair or "artificial" aid. For a time, Mallory had agreed, but as the 1924 team embarked on its final do-or-die attempt, he overrode his scruples to give the expedition its best possible chance.

That change of mind had a crucial bearing on Mallory's choice of partner. Lying in his tent, listening to Mallory, Norton had expected him to nominate the geologist Noel Odell, at 34 one of the most experienced expedition members and still comparatively fit. Instead, Mallory plumped for the Oxford undergraduate "Sandy" Irvine, aged 22, who had proved himself an expert at using the oxygen equipment. Irvine had modified the sets to simplify the oxygen flow and reduced their weight by some 2.3kg (5lb). Although badly affected by sunburn, he readily agreed when Mallory invited him to join the attempt. On the evening of 5 June, Irvine wrote a terse final note in his diary: "My face is perfect agony. Have prepared 2 oxygen apparatus for our start tomorrow morning."

However, they still had to determine the route they would take. The 1924 expedition had already capitalized on the efforts of its predecessors. The 1921 expedition, Mallory to the fore, had identified the North Col as the staging post for attempts on the summit 6,000ft (1,829m) above. The climbers making their attempts in 1922 and earlier in 1924 had followed the line of the broad North Ridge before attempting to traverse the giant North Face, where Norton had gone a short way beyond the Great Couloir that slashed its way down the face. Mallory judged that there was an alternative, namely to ascend to the crest of the Northeast Ridge and follow it to the summit. Although that would ease the route-finding difficulties, it would also mean overcoming two daunting buttresses named the First and Second Steps.

The two men rose early on 6 June, consuming a breakfast of sardines, biscuits, chocolate and tea. Norton, still blind, shook hands with them and wished them good luck. They set out from the North Col around 7.30am, following the broad North Ridge that Mallory had taken with Bruce four days before. They reached Camp V in good time, together with eight porters. Mallory sent four of the porters back to the North Col and on 7 June the group continued to Camp VI at 26,800ft (8,169m), Mallory and Irvine using their oxygen sets during part of the ascent.

After reaching the camp, Mallory wrote two brief letters. One was for John Noel, advising him where to look for them as he and Irvine headed for the summit next day – implying that he had decided to climb to the crest of the Northeast Ridge and tackle the two buttresses or steps. The second was for Odell, apologizing for leaving the camp "in such a mess". He referred to the oxygen equipment, saying "We'll probably go on 2 cylinders," before adding: "It's a bloody load for climbing." Mallory ended on an optimistic note: "Perfect weather for the job".

Mallory gave the letters to the four porters who had accompanied them to Camp VI and were now preparing to descend. When a porter handed Noel his note, he said that the two climbers were well and the weather looked good. The Sherpa porters had been vital to the entire four-year British Everest enterprise. So it is fitting that one of them was the last person to converse with Mallory and Irvine, and then descended bearing Mallory's two final notes.

91

92

91. George Leigh Mallory (1886–1924), photographed by B. Stone.

92. Andrew "Sandy" Irvine (1902–1924), photographed by Mrs Albert Broom.

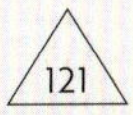

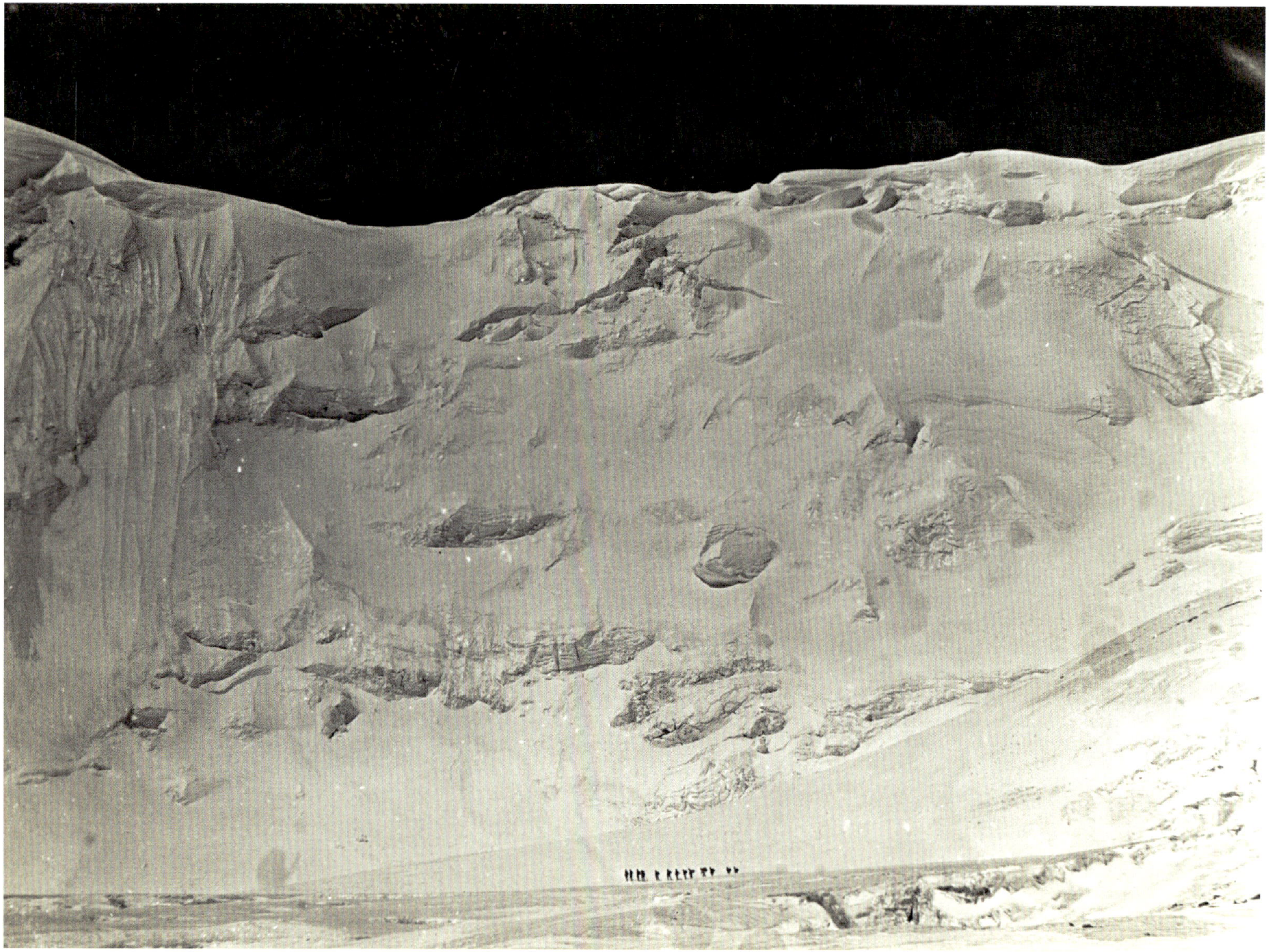

93

93. "Climbing the North Col". A group of climbers in 1924 are dwarfed by the towering ice-wall of the North Col. This was the site of the 1922 disaster when seven porters were killed in an avalanche. Photographed by B. Beetham.

94. "Camp IV on the North Col by a snowy peak." Camp IV was sited on a ledge below the crest of the North Col, giving some protection from the ferocious wind. The photographer, John Noel, dubbed it "Ice Cliff Camp". The photograph shows the ridge of Everest's neighbour Changtse rising beyond giant snow cornices. Photographed by J. B. Noel.

94

95

96

95. Geoffrey Bruce, George Mallory's partner on the 1924 expedition's first summit attempt, photographed at Base Camp with three high-altitude Sherpa porters – so vital to the 1924 team's endeavours.

96. Looking northwest from 24,000ft (7,315m) on Everest. When Edward Norton and Howard Somervell embarked on their summit attempt on 2 June 1924, Somervell took a series of photographs as they went ever higher. The first shows Mount Pumori (23,494 ft, 7,161 m), the triangular peak on the left, rising above the main Rongbuk Glacier. Photographed by T. H. Somervell.

97

97. The summit from 27,000ft (8,230m). Howard Somervell took this photograph from close to Camp V, which he and Edward Norton reached on 3 June 1924. It shows the difficult sloping ground that lay ahead. Photographed by T. H. Somervell.

98. "From 27,500 feet". Taken on the morning of 4 June 1924, this photograph shows that Edward Norton and Howard Somervell could now look down on Mount Pumori, which is prominent in the centre of the frame. Photographed by T. H. Somervell.

98

99

99. "From 28,100 ft". Howard Somervell's highest shot, taken while Edward Norton continued alone, shows the sweeping curve of the North Col at the foot of the frame, with the ridge rising to Changtse on the left. Photographed by T. H. Somervell.

100. "Norton at highest point without oxygen". As Edward Norton went on alone, Howard Somervell photographed him picking his way towards the summit. Norton reached 28,126ft (8,573m) before turning back – an altitude record that stood until 1952 and a record for climbing without supplementary oxygen that was finally exceeded in 1978. Photographed by T. H. Somervell, then image hand-tinted by J. B. Noel.

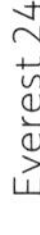

100

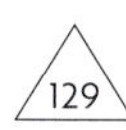

101

Dear Noel
We'll probably start
early to-morrow (8th) in order
to have clear weather. It
won't be too early to start
looking out for us either
crossing the rockband under
the pyramid or going up skyline
at 8.0 p.m.

Yours ever
G Mallory

102

101. Edward Norton and Howard Somervell with the three high-altitude "Tigers" who climbed with them to Camp VI: Norbu Yishe, Lhakpa Chjedi and Semchumbi. Photographed, then hand-tinted, by J. B. Noel.

102. On the eve of his summit attempt, George Mallory sent down a note for John Noel with the Sherpa porters. It read: "Dear Noel, we'll probably start early to-morrow (8th) in order to have clear weather. It won't be too early to start looking out for us either crossing the rock band under the pyramid or going up skyline at 8.0pm. Yours ever, G. Mallory." Mallory was telling Noel where to look out for him and Irvine so he could film or photograph their ascent. The time, 8pm, was clearly a mistake for 8am.

EQUIPMENT AND SUPPLIES

From the collections

The British Mount Everest expeditions of the 1920s are usually seen in headline terms: the personnel, the achievements and the tragedies, but each expedition required meticulous planning to ensure the climbers arrived at Base Camp fit and properly equipped. Of crucial importance was obtaining the right equipment and food supplies for several months. The Mount Everest Committee sourced most necessities in the United Kingdom, but some equipment came from mainland European and India.

Most comestibles, like condensed milk, sardines, Irish stew and Fray Bentos Bully Beef, were supplied by the Army and Navy Cooperative Society. Dried goods included Huntley & Palmer shortbread, Ginger Nut biscuits and Quaker Oats. Four dozen bottles of Montebello Champagne completed the order. Dining utensils were provided by Fortnum & Mason.

Cary Porter and Negretti & Zambra supplied scientific instruments, including aneroid barometers and thermometers. Oxygen equipment came from Siebe Gorman and the British Oxygen Company; Bergans meis og Rygsæk of Norway provided a carrier for transporting the sick or injured; and tents were supplied by Benjamin Edgington. Less vital perhaps, but still a necessity, W. H. Smith provided stationery and a Remington Portable typewriter was gifted by the company.

Clothing was also important and based on the experience gained from previous Everest and Polar expeditions. Windproof clothing was provided by Burberry in the form of their "Shackleton Sledging Outfits" and Cooper, Allen & Co. of Cawnpore provided 22 pairs of boots for the Sherpa porters.

The expedition also provided a marketing opportunity. Sponsorship details and product placements were negotiated. Public interest in the expedition's hero narrative meant companies were keen to see the climbers endorse their brands, with numerous advertisements promoting products as "used by" or "supplied to" the 1924 expedition.

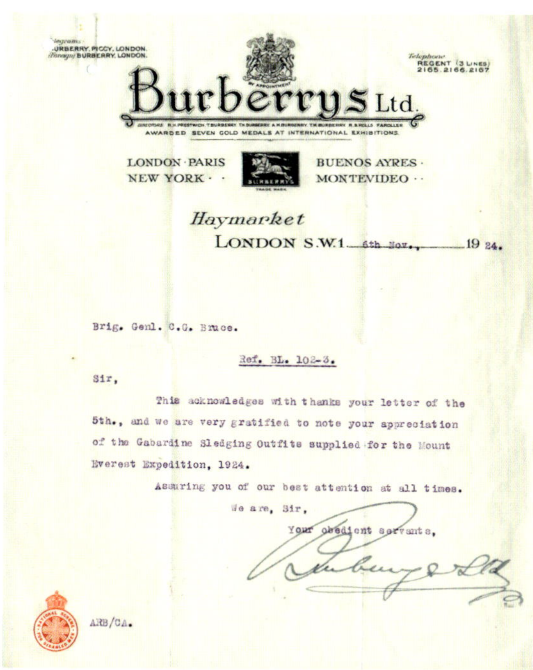

Burberrys Ltd.

Awarded seven gold medals at international exhibitions.

London · Paris · New York · Buenos Ayres · Montevideo

Haymarket
London S.W.1 6th Nov., 1924.

Brig. Genl. C.G. Bruce.

Ref. BL. 102-3.

Sir,

This acknowledges with thanks your letter of the 5th., and we are very gratified to note your appreciation of the Gabardine Sledging Outfits supplied for the Mount Everest Expedition, 1924.

Assuring you of our best attention at all times.

We are, Sir,
Your obedient servants,

Burberrys Ltd

ARB/CA.

104

TELEGRAPHIC ADDRESS: "PARSEE, RAND, LONDON." TELEPHONE GERRARD 3750 (3 LINES)

20 & 21 KING STREET, COVENT GARDEN, W.C.2
AND 25, 26, 31 & 32 BEDFORD STREET, W.C.2
NO OTHER ADDRESS. 6/2/24 19

M A. C. Irvine

PERMANENT ADDRESS 56 Park Rd South Birkenhead

DR. TO MOSS BROS. & CO., LTD.
MILITARY AND GENERAL OUTFITTERS
CLOSE 1 P.M. SATURDAYS

TO BE SENT TO
IT WILL CONSIDERABLY FACILITATE REFERENCE AND ENSURE PROMPT ATTENTION TO ALL COMMUNICATIONS IF THEY BEAR THE NUMBERS QUOTED ON THIS BILL

105

S.O.B.385.

1. Duke Street. London Bridge. S.E.1.
LONDON.

The Mount Everest Committee,
The Royal Geographical Society, 10th December, 1923.

ROYAL 1410.

BOT OF BENJAMIN EDGINGTON,
(S.W. SILVER & Co AND BENJAMIN EDGINGTON, LIMITED)
MARQUEE, TENT, RICK CLOTH, TARPAULIN & FLAG MANUFACTURERS.
COMPLETE OUTFITTERS AND EQUIPMENT CONTRACTORS.

2	Suit Cases, No.5	@ 42/-	4 4 -
	Extra Long Strap and marking	@ 3/-	- 6 -
			£4 10 -

By hand to:-
Kensington Gore,
LONDON, S.W.

NETT

106

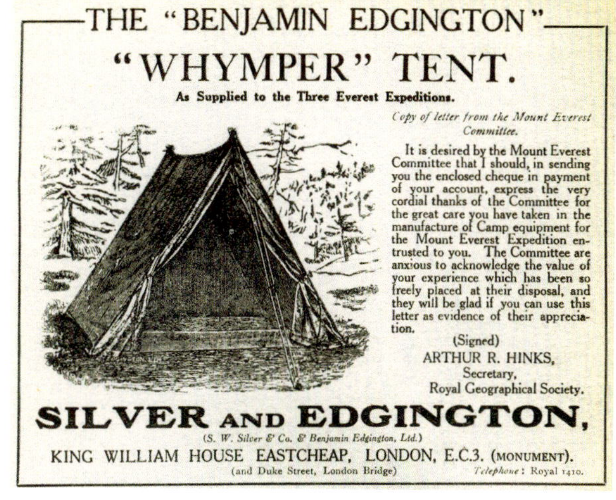

107

103. "No expedition is complete without the Remington Portable". This advertisement appeared in *The Geographical Journal*, March 1926.

104. Letter from Burberrys Ltd to Charles Granville Bruce, 6 November 1924. Bruce had written to Burberrys thanking them for the climbers' outfits, noting they were "excellent in workmanship: it is doubtful that any other material could be found to combine lightness, durability, and resistance to wind so successfully".

105. Moss Bros & Co. invoice for clothing issued to Andrew Irvine and dated 6 February 1924.

106. An invoice for material provided by Benjamin Edgington. They supplied the expedition with suitcases, sleeping bags, mattresses, rucksacks and tables.

107. An advertisement by Silver and Edgington in *The Geographical Journal*, August 1924, promoting the "Whymper Tent" which was supplied to support the 1924 Mount Everest Expedition.

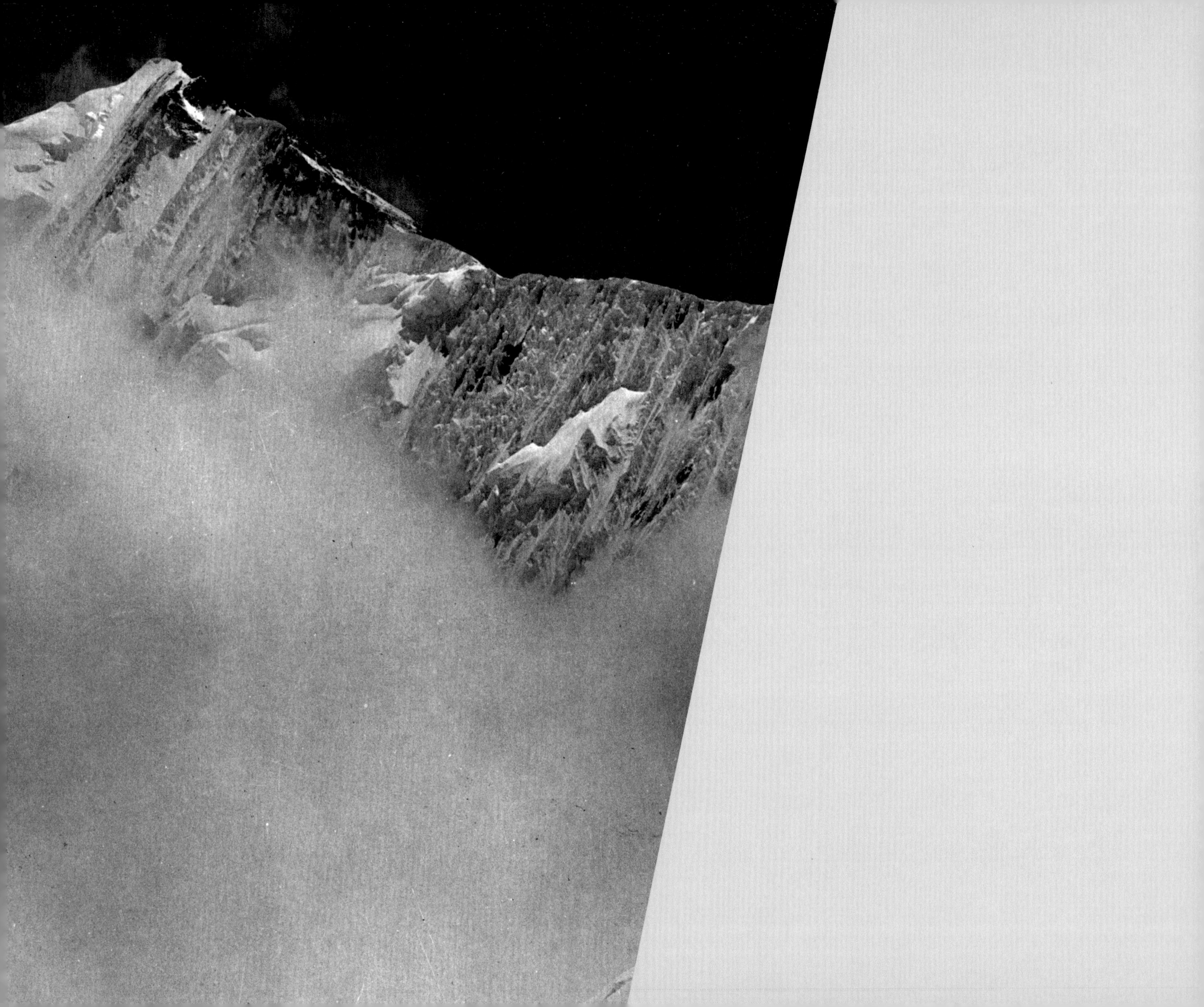

7

24 HOURS

Noel Odell was a geologist who trained at the Royal School of Mines before serving in the Royal Engineers in the First World War. In the early 1920s, he joined the geological staff of the Anglo-Persian Oil Company. Odell's interest in climbing began at the age of 13 and by 26 he had become a member of the Alpine Club. The strength and endurance he demonstrated on the Oxford University expedition to Spitsbergen in 1921 and the Merton College Arctic Expedition in 1923 led to his selection for the 1924 Mount Everest Expedition.

Odell shared joint responsibility for the oxygen equipment with Andrew Irvine on the expedition and acted as support for Mallory and Irvine on the third attempt at the summit. Many, including Edward Norton, thought Odell would have been the preferred choice of climbing partner for Mallory on the grounds of his fitness and climbing experience. However, Mallory planned to make the attempt with oxygen and selected Irvine over Odell due to his skill and initiative in working with the oxygen equipment.

On 6 June 1924, Odell took what was to be the last photograph of Mallory and Irvine as they prepared to set off with eight Sherpa porters from Camp IV (image 108, opposite). During his climb to Camp V in support, Odell famously sighted what he believed to be the pair of climbers progressing up the summit ridge, approaching one of the two "steps", before the scene was enveloped in cloud and the two climbers disappeared behind the mist (image 111, page 141).

Odell's last sighting of Mallory and Irvine ascending the Northeast Ridge left the unanswered question: did Mallory and Irvine reach the summit? As Norton commented: "'Odell alone has carried out the last and hardest task of a supporter – the forlorn-hope search for a party fatally overdue."

108. The last image taken of George Mallory (left) and "Sandy" Irvine as they were about to leave Camp IV on the morning of 6 June 1924 for their summit attempt. Edward Norton lies in one of the tents in the background suffering with severe snow-blindness. Photographed by N. E. Odell.

"We now await news of Mallory and Irvine, who to-day are making another attempt, hoping that they may reinforce the feeble summit air by artificially provided oxygen, and by its means be enabled to conquer the chief difficulty of reaching the summit. May the Genie of the Steel Bottle aid them! All of us are hoping that he may, for nobody deserves the summit more than Mallory..."

– Edward Norton from Camp III on 8 June, "The Mount Everest Dispatches", *The Geographical Journal*, August 1924

A VOICE FROM THE ARCHIVES

Expedition report by Noel Odell

Noel Odell's account of the final fateful 24 hours, recorded in the Society's *Geographical Journal* in December 1924, describes the last contact and sighting of Mallory and Irvine as well as his series of incredible climbs in support and in search of the two climbers.

At 8.40 on the morning of June 6, in brilliant weather, Mallory and Irvine left the North Col Camp for Camp V… On June 7, when they were going from Camp V to VI, I went up in support to Camp V with the one porter that was available.

Next morning broke clear and not unduly cold… I started my solitary climb to Camp VI… At about 25,500 feet I came upon a limestone band which to my joy contained fossils – the first definite forms found on Everest… At about 26,000 feet I climbed a little crag…and as I reached the top there was a sudden clearing above me and I saw the whole summit ridge and final peak of Everest unveiled. I noticed far away on a snow-slope leading up to the last step but one from the base of the final pyramid, a tiny object moving and approaching the rock step. A second object followed, and then the first climbed to the top of the step. As I stood intently watching this dramatic appearance, the scene became enveloped in cloud, and I could not actually be certain that I saw the second figure join the first.

I was surprised above all to see them so late as this, namely 12.50, at a point that according to Mallory's schedule should have been reached by 10 a.m. at latest. I could see they were moving expeditiously as if endeavouring to make up for lost time. True, they were moving at a time over what was apparently but moderately difficult ground, but one cannot definitely conclude from this that they were roped – an important consideration in any estimate of what befell them…

I continued my way up to Camp VI, and on arrival there about two o'clock a rather severe blizzard set in and the wind increased… I realized it was just possible that, baulked by earlier bad weather higher up, Mallory and Irvine might be returning, and the concealed position of Camp VI would be almost impossible to discover in the blizzard… So I went out in the direction of the summit, and having scrambled up about 200 feet… yodelled and whistled…

After about an hour's wait, realizing that the chances were altogether against their being within call, I found my way back to the tent. As I reached it the storm, which had lasted not more than two hours, blew over, and the whole north face of the mountain became bathed in sunshine. The upper crags were visible, but I could see no signs of the party… Leaving Camp VI…about 4.30 and going down the north ridge in quick time, I took to the snow near Camp V and glissaded down to the North Col, reaching the camp at 6.45… We watched till late that night for some signs of Mallory and Irvine's return, or even an indication by flare of distress.

Next morning we scrutinized through field glasses the tiny tents of Camps V and VI far up above us in case they had returned late and had not yet started down. But no movement at all could be seen.

At noon I decided to go up to Camp V, and on to VI next day… On reaching the tent at VI I found everything as I had left it: the tent had obviously not been touched since I was there two days previously…

After a couple of hours' search I realized that the chances of finding the missing men were indeed small on such a vast expanse of crags and broken slabs… I returned only too reluctantly to the tent, and then with considerable exertion dragged the two sleeping-bags up a precipitous snow patch… With these sleeping-bags placed against the snow I had arranged with Hazard to signal down to the North Col Camp the results of my search…fortunately the signal was seen 4,000 feet below…

…I must now very briefly speculate on the probable causes of their failure to return. They had about 800 feet to surmount to reach the top, and if no particularly difficult obstacle presented itself on the final pyramid they should have got there about 3 to 3.30. This would be three or four hours late on Mallory's schedule, and hence they would find it almost impossible to reach Camp VI before nightfall… But at the same time it must be remembered there was a moon… In spite of this they may have missed the way and failed to find Camp VI, and in their overwrought condition sought shelter till daylight…sleep at that altitude and in that degree of cold would almost certainly prove fatal.

The other possibility is that they met their death by falling. This implies that they were roped together… It is difficult for one who knew the skill and experience of George Mallory on all kinds and conditions of mountain ground, to believe that he fell… They were hampered of course by the oxygen apparatus – a very serious load for climbing with… But could such a pair fall, and where technically the climbing appeared so easy?

109

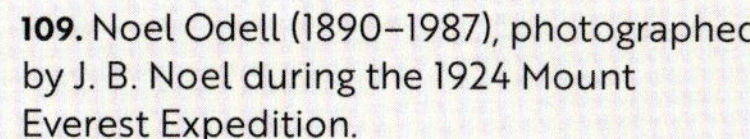

109. Noel Odell (1890–1987), photographed by J. B. Noel during the 1924 Mount Everest Expedition.

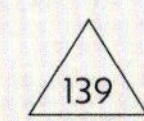

...It has been suggested that the oxygen apparatus failed and thereby rendered them powerless to return. I cannot believe this...to be deprived of oxygen at any rate when one has not been using it freely does not prevent one from continuing, and, least of all, getting down from the mountain... Hence I incline to the view first expressed, that they met their death by being benighted. I know that Mallory had stated he would take risks in any attempt on the final peak... The knowledge of his own proved powers of endurance, and those of his companion, may have urged him to make a bold bid for the summit...

The question remains: "Has Mount Everest been climbed?" It must be left unanswered, for there is no evidence. But bearing in mind all the circumstances that I have set out above, and considering their position when last seen, I myself feel it is very probable that Mallory and Irvine succeeded. At that I must leave it.

110

110. "Gneiss with pegmatite veins (light) – Irvine, Beetham and Mallory". Noel Odell was a geologist and trained at the Royal School of Mines, and following the 1924 Mount Everest Expedition became lecturer of Geology at Harvard University from 1928 to 1930. During the expedition, Odell made extensive observations of the geology of the Tibetan Plateau and Himalayan mountains and was the first to collect samples of fossils on Everest. Photographed by N. E. Odell.

111. Illustration of Noel Odell watching for Mallory and Irvine and the location of the First and Second Positions (Steps), where Odell believed he sighted the climbers through the mist. Drawn by D. Macpherson, 1924.

111

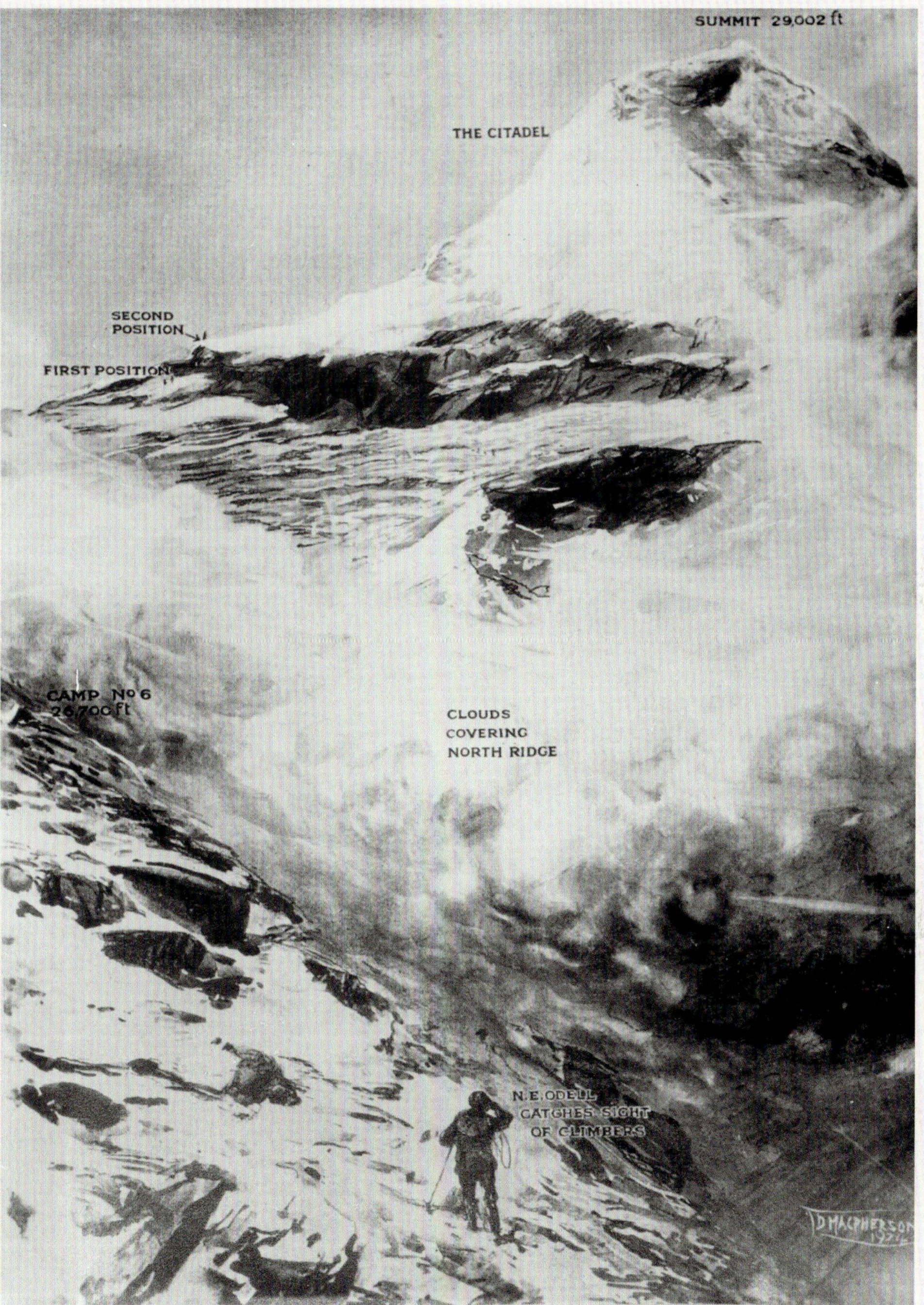

112

112. "Chang La – Odell and porters". The 1924 Mount Everest Expedition was Noel Odell's first Himalayan expedition. It is remarkable that, in support and in search of Mallory and Irvine, he stayed at an altitude over 7,000m for 11 nights and made two lone searches for the lost climbers up to 26,903ft (8,200m). Photographed by J. de V. Hazard.

113. "Camp IV on the North Col". Camp IV was used by a support party of two climbers during the summit attempts. Photographed by J. B. Noel.

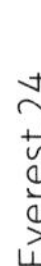

113

114

114. "Looking south-southeast from Camp IV – Noel with camera". John Noel travelled between camps to film the progress of the climbers. Photographed by J. de V. Hazard.

115. "The summit of Mount Everest shrouded in cloud and taken with a telephoto lens". John Noel used a specially designed telephoto lens from the lower camps to take detailed photographs of the summit and record the climbers' progress. Photographed by J. B. Noel.

115

116

117

116. "Khartaphu and Upper East Rongbuk Glacier from the North Col". Photographed by A. C. Irvine. Although Andrew Irvine, at the age of 22, had limited mountaineering experience, Edward Norton wrote how he was a valued member of the team, "able to hold his own with all modesty on terms at least of equality with the other members of our party", and that his "cheerful camaraderie, his unselfishness and high courage made him loved, not only by all of us, but also by the porters".

117. A photograph showing George Mallory and Andrew Irvine's progress towards the summit of Everest, indicating the point at which Noel Odell believed that he sighted the climbers. Photographed, then hand-tinted, by J. B. Noel.

118

118. On returning to Base Camp, Howard Somervell and Bentley Beetham supervised the building of a memorial cairn that bears the names of Mallory, Irvine, Man Bahadur and Shamsherpun, along with those of others lost in previous Everest expeditions. These included Alexander Kellas in 1921 and the seven Sherpa porters who died in the avalanche on the 1922 expedition: Lhakpa, Narbu, Pasang, Pemba, Sange, Temba and Antarge. Photographed by J. B. Noel, 1924.

119. Letter from George Mallory's widow, Ruth, to Geoffrey Winthrop Young, a climbing mentor and close friend of Mallory's, following the news of the death of her husband. In the letter Ruth Mallory writes: "I know so absolutely that he could not have failed in courage or self sacrifice. Whether he got to the top of the mountain or did not, whether he lived or died makes no difference to my admiration for him... Oh Geoffrey, if only it hadn't happened! It so easily might not have."

Westbrook
Godalming
3/5/19

My dear Geoffrey

I am very grateful to you for you long and thoughtful letter. I think I do understand it. You are quite right. I know George did not mean to be killed, he meant not to be so hard that I did not a bit think he would be. I know this is not an answer to what you said. I dont think I do feel that his death makes me the least more proud of him. It is his life that I loved & love. I know so absolutely that he could not have failed in courage or self sacrifice. Whether he got to the top of the mountain or did not, whether he lived or died makes no difference to my admiration for him. I think I have got the pain separate. There is so much of it and it will go on so long that I must do that. I am sending you the last letter I have had from George. You will find it very interesting. There will I think certainly be one more after this. I may get it tomorrow. You shall have the climbing part of it in due course.

Oh Geoffrey. If only it hadn't happened. It so easily might not have.

Yours
Ruth Mallory

119

MALLORY'S ARTEFACTS

From the collections

Noel Odell's report of his last sighting of Mallory and Irvine was doubted by many from the climbing community; they believed it was more likely he'd seen the pair climbing the easier First Step, rather than the Second Step. The pressure led Odell to question his sighting, and he later admitted he could no longer be certain at which of the steps he had seen them. However, some climbers, including Edward Norton, thought it highly possible that Mallory and Irvine may have reached the summit.

Numerous theories and speculation have surrounded the mystery of their disappearance ever since, but it wasn't until the 1930s that the first clues were found. Percy Wyn-Harris, a member of Hugh Ruttledge's 1933 Mount Everest Expedition, found an ice axe, believed to belong to Mallory or Irvine, lying on a rock slab, just short of the First Step, considerably lower than Odell's last sighting of them.

In 1975 Wang Hong-Bao, a Chinese climber, reported seeing the body of a fallen climber at about 27,000ft (8,230m), near Camp VI. On a Sino-Japanese expedition four years later, Wang shared the information with a Japanese climber, Hasegawa Ryoten Yashimoro, but tragically the Chinese climber died the following day and details of the exact location were lost.

Mallory's body was eventually discovered on 1 May 1999, 75 years after his disappearance, at 26,800ft (8,169m) and in the same area Wang had described. Irvine's body has never been found. The "Mallory and Irvine Research Expedition", led by Eric Simonsen and sponsored by the American Foundation for International Mountaineering, Exploration and Research (AFFIMER), had also hoped to find a Kodak Vest Pocket camera, which, if preserved and intact, could contain photographic evidence of whether they did indeed reach the summit of Everest.

120

122

121

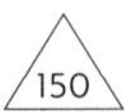

124

125

123

120. A pair of goggles found in George Mallory's pocket.

121. Mallory's hobnail boot.

122. Mallory's wristwatch.

123. Mallory's handkerchief with monogram "GLM" (George Leigh Mallory).

124. Mallory's altimeter.

125. Climbing rope fragment.

1

8

FILM & PHOTOGRAPHY

The work of photographing the 1924 Mount Everest Expedition was principally undertaken by John Noel and Bentley Beetham, the former by plan and the latter by chance. Beetham was a friend of Howard Somervell, a member of the 1922 Mount Everest Expedition. Both excellent climbers, together they made many ascents of classic routes in the English Lakes.

Unfortunately for Beetham, he contracted dysentery as the 1924 expedition moved through Sikkim and, on recovery, he then suffered a severe attack of sciatica. The expedition was denied his climbing skills, but Beetham was determined to contribute to the expedition through his photography.

John Noel had filmed the 1922 expedition and again planned to film the 1924 expedition, buying the rights from the Mount Everest Committee (MEC) to do so. The MEC had been pleased with the results of his filming of the 1922 expedition and so was happy for Noel to film the summit attempt again in 1924. Noel brought with him a focus on storytelling that would both promote and monetize the expedition in the way that Frank Hurley had done with his film of Ernest Shackleton's *Endurance* expedition (1914–17) just a few years before.

Both Beetham and Noel would produce spectacular records of the 1924 climb, but it was Noel's entrepreneurial instincts that would lead to some unexpected tensions within both the expedition and the MEC.

John Noel was a true innovator in both photography and cinematography. He refined the equipment he used, learning lessons from the likes of Herbert Ponting, Robert Falcon Scott's photographer on the *Terra Nova* expedition (1910–13). His adventurous spirit and flair for capturing the most descriptive and dramatic images is shown in the photograph here of Noel filming on scree slopes with a telephoto lens (image 131, page 161), and must be seen in the same vein as Frank Hurley's stunning photographic record of the *Endurance* expedition led by Shackleton. The quality of Noel's photography and films help to explain why the expeditions resonated so much with Western audiences.

"[John Noel] must be congratulated most warmly upon the result of a remarkable effort of endurance and skill…it wants a very good man to attend to the many details required of a kinematographer operating with an enormous telephoto lens in camp for four days and nights at 23,000 feet, with the added responsibility of commanding the supports for the high-climbing party above him."

– "The Mount Everest Kinematograph Film", *The Geographical Journal*, 1923

126. The summit of Mount Everest. Photograph taken by John Noel and later hand-tinted. On returning from the expedition, Noel hand-tinted his slides with the ambition of introducing his audience to the colours witnessed "at the top of the world".

NOEL AND HIS "FANTASTIC WAY OF DOING THINGS"

Essay by Dr Jan Faull

A unique set of circumstances surrounded the commissioning of films to record the progress of the 1922 and 1924 Mount Everest expeditions. Arthur Hinks, Secretary of the Mount Everest Committee (MEC), had a profound dislike of all commercial media and only entered into negotiations with the press because of the necessity of raising funds for the expeditions. His particular distrust of the film industry was instrumental in the appointment of John Baptist Lucius Noel as official cinematographer in 1922.

In spite of recommendations from John Buchan, all pitches from leading British production companies were dismissed in favour of Noel, a Fellow of the Royal Geographical Society and a Captain in the East Yorkshire Regiment, who was serving in India. Hinks was aware of Noel's ambitions to travel through Tibet to Everest and of his interest in photography and hoped that by appointing him he would be governed by a code of conduct, which could possibly have been more difficult to oversee with the appointment of an independent film company.

With no history of commissioning film or managing the exhibition and distribution of the end result, the MEC relied on the traditional route of the lecture circuit, with members of the climbing party enlisted to present their experiences and a separate film exhibition taking a secondary role. No one could anticipate the results of the expedition (it was regarded primarily as a scientific venture), let alone the results that could be achieved filming at such an extremely high altitude. No specific plans for independent screenings were drawn up in advance, which Noel found very frustrating. Eventually Noel and Hinks were forced into managing the exhibition of the film, *Climbing Mount Everest*, an extra burden that Hinks found very onerous.

The 1922 expedition had been a steep learning curve. Noel had followed the work of Herbert Ponting in filming Captain Robert Scott's failed attempt to reach the South Pole. Using similar Newman Sinclair 35mm camera equipment, adapted to film at high altitude, he processed the flammable nitrate film stock in a photographic tent at Base Camp, drying the film at night over a smouldering fire of yak dung. He experienced problems with static when filming and dust adhering to the surface of the exposed film – both not anticipated. Thus, provided with first-hand experience of the pitfalls of filming in extreme conditions, he could revise his plans.

Revenue was an important factor and Noel determined on an efficient business plan. He decided to finance the filming of the 1924 expedition by raising £8,000 from private investors. He set up his own company, Explorers Films, and negotiated control of the rights and management of all film and photography. He could therefore issue the members of the expedition with a schedule of expectations. Although Hinks and Noel continued to correspond over the progress of the expedition, control of the filming and management of outcomes had been relinquished. The very anxieties that Hinks had felt over engaging a commercial production company would come back to haunt him. Noel now became the entrepreneur, embracing available opportunities to harness promotional methods and new technological developments.

Noel's unorthodox plans met with varying success. Rather than processing film in Tibet, he organized the building of a bespoke film laboratory in Darjeeling. This was managed by Arthur Pereira, Honorary Secretary of the Royal Photographic Society, who would be in charge of processing the rushes (raw film footage from the day's shoot). These were carried down the 100-plus miles to Darjeeling by relays of runners. Pereira also produced a series of silent news items for Pathé News, thus maintaining public awareness of the expedition's progress.

Noel had followed attempts to introduce colour on film and the coincidental showing of the experimental Friese-Greene Natural Colour Process at the Holborn Empire in London, just prior to departure for India, provided a press opportunity. Various news items appeared with headlines such as "What Colours are at the Top of the World", creating the expectation of a colour film production. In fact, the process, adding blue-green and red tints to sequential frames of film and projecting at double speed, was only at an experimental stage and Noel's rather impetuous embracing of the technology proved premature. More traditional methods of adding colour tints to sections of his final edit would provide atmosphere and interest. His colour glass slides would compensate on the lecture circuit.

127

127. An advertisement from *The Geographical Journal* in October 1924, titled "Everest 1924 The NS Kine' Camera Again Successful", which includes a quote from John Noel endorsing the camera and a photograph of Noel filming on the North Peak with his camera and telephoto lens.

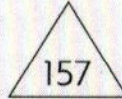

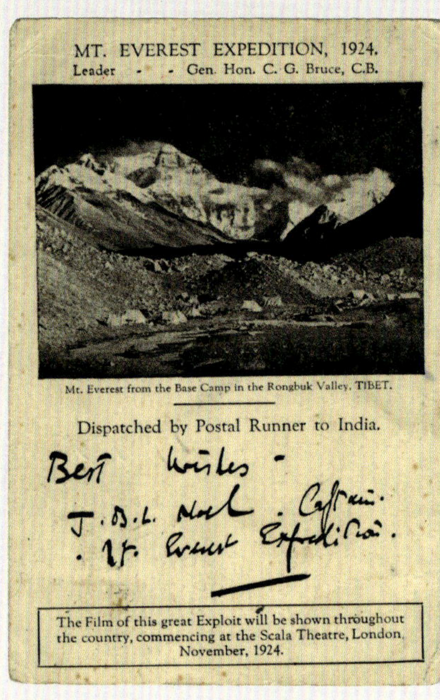

128

Another such "scheme" was the attempt to film the progress of the party across the Tibetan Plateau, using a Citroën Kégresse tractor. The tractor, not surprisingly, was abandoned shortly after setting off. More success was achieved by the sale of postcards, complete with a specially designed stamp, sent from Base Camp. A series of cigarette cards to collect would follow.

During the initial stages, the party was accompanied by Noel's wife, Sybille, and the artist Francis Helps. Sybille collected folk tales, later published as *The Magic Bird of Chomo-Lung-Ma*. Helps produced a series of portraits of Tibetans encountered en route, as well as designing the stamp for the Everest postcard.

The loss of Mallory and Irvine put paid to a triumphal film – Noel had to adapt his material and concentrate on the mystery of the mountain itself – "a 'something' which would make the spectator feel the immensity of this struggle of Man against Nature… To dabble fatuously in trivialities in face of Everest's grandeur would be sacrilege."

In advance of his return from India, Noel organized a grand theatrical spectacle at the New Scala Theatre in London, *The Epic of Everest*, which was billed as "A Wonder Film of Adventure on the Roof of the World". A backdrop, designed by Joseph Harker, decorated the theatre, a group of Tibetan monks appeared on stage, a quartet led by Eugene Goossens provided musical accompaniment, and Noel himself gave a commentary in the interval. The monks assumed celebrity status wherever they appeared – not in their best interests – as the diplomatic row over "The Affair of the Dancing Lamas" would later prove (see page 174).

Noel had let his impulsive entrepreneurial activities run riot. Although these promotional activities were seen as outside Noel's remit by many, his innovative use of film technology cannot be denied. Sequences using a 20-inch Cooke telephoto lens – filming scenes at a distance of over two miles – all combined to produce a film that was heralded by film critics. As Iris Barry wrote:

> *…the picture has magnificently that rare quality of communication through the visual sense which is one of the particular qualities of the cinema; it communicates an experience which almost none of us can ever have in fact.*

Once the initial theatrical season finished, a series of provincial performances went on tour, followed by European venues. Noel, avoiding fallout from the diplomatic problems surrounding his film, explored new opportunities to repurpose content. He embarked on a series of lectures across America which secured him a role as a travelling lecturer/showman. Hinks gave him permission to combine material from both his Everest films to create lecture content. A subsequent expedition to Kashmir, funded by Harvard University, with Alfred Raetz, the lantern colourist, in 1929, provided new film and photographic records to incorporate with his Everest material. In 1931 a sound film *The Tragedy of Everest*, with narration by American actor David Ross, was released. No physical copy survives, only a vibrant colour poster found in Noel's paperwork.

Throughout his long life Noel continued to lecture on the 1924 climb, using his material to great effect. Arthur Hinks had felt powerless to intervene when questioned about Noel's activities, only referring to them as "Noel's fantastic way of doing things". When permission to mount a new expedition was granted in 1933, the MEC announced that no official cinematographer would be appointed. However, by then new lighter 16mm equipment enabled individual climbers to film their own records. Noel continued to explore film technology as new formats evolved, expressing a wish that his colour stills should be edited into his film to make it "worthy of a national record".

129

128. A postcard sent by John Noel from Base Camp, promoting the film screening of *The Epic of Everest* at the Scala Theatre in November 1924. The verso of the postcard is stamped "Rongbuk Glacier Base Camp, Mt. Everest Expedition, 1924".

129. A poster for *The Epic of Everest*, John Noel's film of the 1924 Mount Everest Expedition. Following the death of George Mallory and Andrew Irvine, and the expedition's failure to reach the summit, Noel was forced to reconfigure his original documentary film plans.

130

130. John Noel photographed and filmed both the 1922 and 1924 Mount Everest expeditions. Here, he is seen kinematographing the Everest ascent from the Chang La in 1922. One of his Sherpa porters steadies the tripod behind. Previously credited to Noel but most likely taken by a Sherpa porter.

131. Noel's photographic porters were vital to filming at altitude; they assisted Noel and carried the cameras and other heavy photographic equipment up difficult and dangerous mountainous terrain. Photographed by J. B. Noel during the 1924 Mount Everest Expedition.

131

132

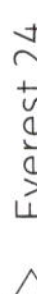

132. A photograph of Camp IV, the North Col Camp, Mount Everest Expedition, 1924. John Noel recorded the colours of every still photograph he took on the expedition, so that once converted to glass slides, they could be faithfully tinted by hand.

133. A promotional brochure for John Noel's film *The Epic of Everest* (1924). The film is advertised as "A Wonder Film of Adventure on the Roof of the World".

133

ASTRA NATIONAL

present

(By arrangement with A. E. Bundy and Peter Taylor)

CAPT. J. B. NOEL'S PRODUCTION

The Epic of Everest

A Wonder Film of Adventure on the Roof of the World

The Men of the Expedition :

General the Hon. C. G. BRUCE, C.B. - -	*Leader*
GEOFFREY BRUCE - - - -	*Climber*
BENTLEY BEETHAM - - - -	,,
H. HAZARD - - - - -	,,
R. W. H. HINGSTON - - -	*Doctor and Naturalist*
M. IRVINE - - - - -	*Climber*
M. G. LEIGH MALLORY - - -	,,
Capt. J. B. NOEL, F.R.G.S. - - -	*Photographer*
Col. E. F. NORTON - -	*Climber (Second in Command)*
N. E. ODELL - - - - -	*Climber*
E. O. SHEBBEARE - - -	*Transport and Baggage*
HOWARD SOMERVELL - - -	*Climber*

134

134. A still taken from John Noel's film *The Epic of Everest* (1924). Scenes from the film show the overladen porters at the start of the expedition. The intertitle script describes the porters as "the sturdiest mountaineers in the Himalayas".

135. A still taken from John Noel's film *The Epic of Everest* (1924). This image shows Sherpa porters using a telescope to search for the missing climbers.

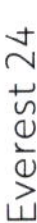

135

136

136. A film poster for John Noel's *The Tragedy of Everest* (1931), which combined footage from both the 1922 and 1924 Mount Everest expeditions.

137. A promotional flyer for John Noel's later provincial lecture, "Through Tibet to Everest", at the Winter Gardens, Eastbourne.

THROUGH TIBET TO EVEREST
TOLD & ILLUSTRATED on the SCREEN IN COLOUR PICTURES BY
CAPT. JOHN NOEL
AUTHOR OF "THROUGH TIBET TO EVEREST" & "THE STORY OF EVEREST"
OFFICIAL PHOTOGRAPHER TO 2 OF THE PIONEER MT. EVEREST EXPEDITIONS OF THE ROYAL GEOGRAPHICAL SOCIETY.
WINTER GARDEN EASTBOURNE.
MANAGEMENT MR GEORGE HILL.
THUR. 2ND FEB. at 3 & 8 P.M.
TICKETS 3/6 & 2/6 BOX OFFICE EASTBOURNE 5252.
L. STONER.
24 STATION LANE,
HORNCHURCH.

137

HAND-TINTED SLIDES AND THE COLOUR DISSOLVOGRAPH

From the collections

John Noel's collection of hand-tinted glass sides is exceptional. The quality equals the autochrome process employed in the collection of Albert Kahn's *Archives of the Planet*. In the 1920s, the introduction of colour to black and white images was an added attraction for audiences eager to experience the expeditionary journey. Noel's ambition was to introduce the many vibrant colours witnessed en route to Mount Everest – the variety of colours seen in the flora and fauna, religious ceremonies and Tibetan culture, as well as in the terrain and portraits of the climbing party. He laboriously recorded all the colours seen during the journey so that later, using colour charts and specialist lantern slide watercolours, he could add the appropriate shades to his monochrome images. He specifically described the resulting images as being "all my own work".

During Noel's initial lecture tours in North America in the mid-1920s he met and subsequently worked with celebrated American lantern colourist Alfred Raetz. Undoubtedly, he benefitted from Raetz's expertise in producing further lecture material. Noel also developed improvements in the delivery of the colour slides. Reviews of Noel's lectures invariably praise the colours and seamless delivery achieved by the use of "the colour dissolvograph". Although the glass slides are now preserved at the Royal Geographical Society, all that remains of the dissolvograph lantern modification are the impressive reviews found in press coverage and promotional advertising. For example, a glowing endorsement from the Detroit Institute of Arts reads, "I was amazed and delighted at the wonderful colouring and artistry of his pictures. Our audience was wildly enthusiastic."

The elderly Noel was still giving benefit lectures in his home county of Kent well into the 1970s, using his slides to great effect, which illustrates the lasting appreciation of an obsolete form.

138

138. "The Dzongpen of Kharta and his wife". This image was originally photographed by Charles Howard-Bury on the 1921 Mount Everest Reconnaissance Expedition. It was then hand-tinted by John Noel in 1924.

139. Shekar monastery, 1924 Mount Everest Expedition. Photographed and hand-tinted by John Noel, 1924.

140. Rongbuk Monastery with Mount Everest in the background. Photographed and hand-tinted by John Noel, 1924.

141. "Second days' camp in Arun valley, where track ended". This photograph was taken by C. J. Morris on the 1922 expedition and later hand-tinted by John Noel.

142. A path through a forested valley, taken on the 1922 Mount Everest Expedition. John Noel meticulously hand-tinted the slide with the colours of the vegetation and flowers.

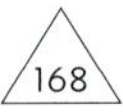

139

140

141

142

THE LEGACY

The legacy of the 1924 Mount Everest Expedition took many forms. The first and most immediate response from the Royal Geographical Society (RGS), the Alpine Club, the Mount Everest Committee (MEC) and the public in Britain and across the world was one of grief that George Mallory and Andrew Irvine had died pushing for the summit.

The MEC received telegrams and letters of condolence from across the globe, including a telegram sent by King George V:

> *The King is greatly distressed to hear the sad news of the death of Mr. Mallory and Mr. Irvine who lost their lives in making a final attempt to reach the summit of Mount Everest.*
>
> *His Majesty asks whether you will be good enough to convey to the families of those two gallant explorers as well as to the Mount Everest Committee an expression of his sincere sympathy.*

This outpouring of grief sets in stark contrast the absence of any note of condolence for the seven porters who perished in an avalanche in 1922 or the two who tragically died in 1924.

The dramatic end to the expedition and the expression of public grief led to greater interest in John Noel's film of the expedition, *The Epic of Everest* (1924), which broke new ground in documentary filmmaking. However, the theatrical performance arranged by Noel as a prologue to the film, would have serious consequences for Anglo–Tibetan relations and future Mount Everest expeditions.

The music and dance performances of the Tibetan people were of special interest to the Western expedition members as they travelled to the mountain. The photographic collections of these early expeditions contain a profusion of images, including George Mallory's record of a formal dance at Rongbuk Monastery (image 149, page 179) and Charles John Morris's photograph of the traditional dress worn by folk musicians (image 150, page 180).

"[George Mallory and Andrew Irvine] will ever be remembered as fine examples of mountaineers – ready to risk their lives for their own companions and to face dangers on behalf of science and discovery."

– King George V, *Telegram to the Mount Everest Committee*, 1924

143. Tibetan dancers in traditional dress. Photographed by J. B. Noel.

143

THE MANY FACES OF A MOUNTAIN

Essay by Dr Peter H. Hansen

After the return of the 1924 Mount Everest Expedition, Mallory and Irvine were mourned at St Paul's Cathedral, celebrated at the Albert Hall and projected on cinema screens across Great Britain. John Noel's film *The Epic of Everest* opened in London with a live prologue featuring Lhakpa Tsering, a Sherpa porter at Mallory and Irvine's highest camps, and music, chants and dances performed by a group of seven Buddhist monks from a monastery at Gyantse, Tibet. Controversies over these "dancing lamas" led to a breakdown in Anglo–Tibetan relations and the cancellation of Mount Everest expeditions for almost a decade. The expedition and film also illustrate the enduring intercultural consequences of the 1924 Mount Everest Expedition, which extended from Britain to the Himalayas.

Noel's film depicted a cinematic struggle of inquisitive white men against a mystical mountain. After the tragic deaths of Mallory and Irvine, the film asked whether Everest was more than a mountain of rock and ice and snow, but alive and guarded by the spirit of Chomo-lung-ma (Goddess Mother of the World): "Strangely to memory the words of the Rongbuk Lama come: 'The Gods of the Lamas shall deny you White Men the object of your search.'" The film then closed with close-ups of the Rongbuk Lama followed by time-lapsed views of clouds, sunset and Chomolungma from the monastery as darkness falls.

The visit of the "dancing lamas" brought this narrative to life and created a sensation in London. Much of the British press adopted a tone of superiority and mocked the lamas' visits to the zoo, shops and a Punch and Judy show. They also misconstrued their reaction to London as a fear of technology and "white man's magic". The Head Lama, Gana Suta Chenpo, told *The Times* he regretted so few people did any real work in London, since they relied on machinery and would be destroyed by their machines. Rinchen Lhamo, a Tibetan woman living in London, recognized this critique as the remark of an acute observer and wondered whether journalists could not understand it due to orientalist stereotypes that Tibetans were primitive.

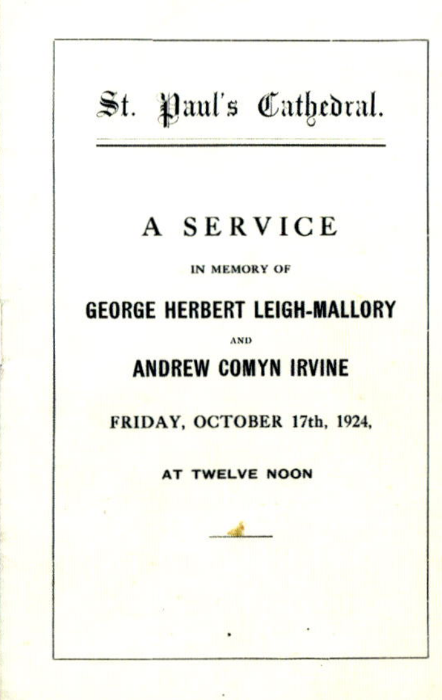
St. Paul's Cathedral.

A SERVICE

IN MEMORY OF

GEORGE HERBERT LEIGH-MALLORY

AND

ANDREW COMYN IRVINE

FRIDAY, OCTOBER 17th, 1924,

AT TWELVE NOON

144

Leaders of Tibet, Sikkim and Bhutan were offended in various ways – by scenes in the film, the expedition's unauthorised detours in Tibet, and newspaper photographs of the "dancing lamas". Indeed, officials from Sikkim and Bhutan saw the film in Darjeeling and objected to scenes that were later cut. The climbers had also travelled beyond the areas authorized by their climbing permits. While Tibetan officials forgave the climbers' trespasses in Tibet, in 1925 they regarded taking the monks to London as "very unbecoming. For the future, we cannot give them permission to go to Tibet." The Dalai Lama saw pictures of the "dancing lamas" in newspapers and viewed the affair as an affront to Tibetan Buddhism.

The "dancing lamas" also played a decisive role in undermining the reputation of the military in Tibet. In 1921, Tibet had given permission for the first Everest expedition in exchange for British weapons. The dancing lamas controversy was one of several events in 1924–25 that tipped the balance of power in Tibet from the military to the monasteries. When border conflicts escalated in the 1930s, Tibet again turned to the British for weapons and began giving Everest climbing permits as welcoming gifts to British envoys visiting Lhasa. The Tibetan military never recovered from the loss of support from the Tibetan elites in the 1920s and it was too weak to stop invading forces in the 1950s.

Elsewhere in the Himalayas, the porters returning from the 1924 Mount Everest Expedition inspired others to follow in their footsteps. Ang Tharkay and Tenzing Norgay became porters on Everest after hearing about the 1924 expedition and later took leadership roles on Annapurna and Everest. One of Ang Tharkay's friends returned from Everest to Khunde, in Nepal, strutting about with his climbing gear as if he had accomplished something awe-inspiring. Tharkay remarked: "As I was younger than he was, my imagination ran wild when I heard his sensational description of his adventures. I was so impressed that I immediately felt an uncontrollable

145

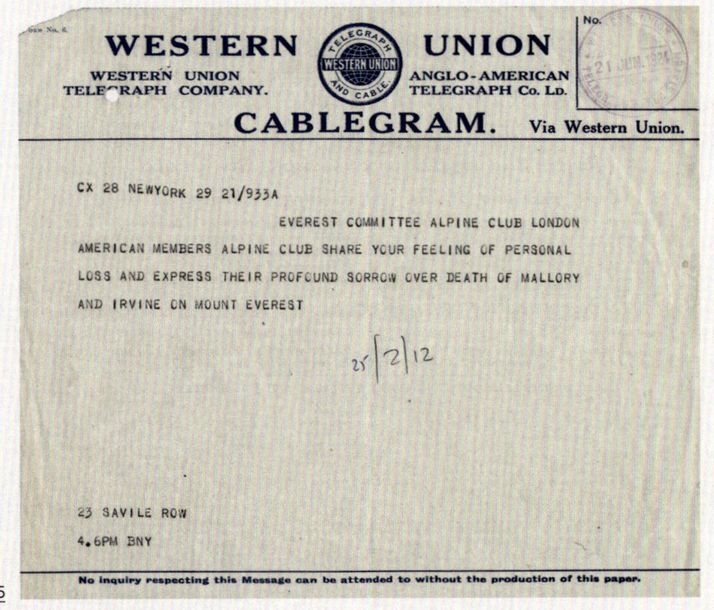
WESTERN UNION

WESTERN UNION TELEGRAPH COMPANY. — ANGLO-AMERICAN TELEGRAPH Co. Ld.

CABLEGRAM. Via Western Union.

No.

CX 28 NEWYORK 29 21/933A

EVEREST COMMITTEE ALPINE CLUB LONDON

AMERICAN MEMBERS ALPINE CLUB SHARE YOUR FEELING OF PERSONAL LOSS AND EXPRESS THEIR PROFOUND SORROW OVER DEATH OF MALLORY AND IRVINE ON MOUNT EVEREST

25/2/12

23 SAVILE ROW

4.6PM BNY

No inquiry respecting this Message can be attended to without the production of this paper.

144. Cover of the printed order of service held in memory of George Mallory and Andrew Irvine on 17 October 1924 at St Paul's Cathedral, London.

145. A telegram from the American Alpine Club expressing their sorrow at the death of George Mallory and Andrew Irvine. The outpouring of grief and sorrow was immense as news of their tragic death spread across the globe; there was little mention of the tragic death of the two porters during the same expedition.

146

desire to follow his example and to try to join an expedition myself." Tenzing Norgay developed the same ambition after hearing stories about big boots, strange clothes and Everest. "What is Everest?" Tenzing asked. "It is the same as Chomolungma," replied Sherpas who had climbed on its other side, in Tibet.

Collaborative expeditions to Everest initiated in the 1920s were crowned by the first ascent by Tenzing Norgay and Edmund Hillary in 1953. After reaching the summit, Tenzing and Hillary both looked for traces of Mallory and Irvine but could not see any. Tenzing recalled hearing the names of Mallory and Irvine in the 1920s and never forgot them. They descended to Camp IV where the 1953 film crew recorded their joyous reunion and celebrated the teamwork of Sherpas and Sahibs alike, and all who had come before. Amid the celebrations, Hillary told one of the other climbers, Wilfred Noyce, "Wouldn't Mallory be pleased if he knew about this?"

Climbers from around the world have been fascinated by the fate of Mallory and Irvine. Chinese climbers made the first ascent of Chomolungma from the north in 1960. When they climbed the route again in 1975, a Chinese climber reported seeing the body of "English dead". On the north side in 1980, Italian mountaineer Reinhold Messner had visions, heard voices and sensed the spirit of Mallory and Irvine during his solo ascent of Everest without bottled oxygen. Even after the discovery of Mallory's body in 1999, the fate of Mallory and Irvine has remained the subject of continuing speculation along with search parties funded by cinematic reenactments and commercial documentaries.

All too often, the 1924 expedition is remembered as a "pure" adventure before Everest became crowded and commercial. Nostalgia for lost colonial privileges is one of the expedition's legacies. But nostalgia should not obscure the deeply commercial character of the 1924 Mount Everest Expedition, which was funded by John Noel's film company and publicized by orientalist images of white men overcoming superstitions in Tibet. Reactions to the interplay of climbing and commerce were as intense then as they are now, a century later. The worldly connections set in motion on Everest in 1924 are still at work among us.

146. A promotional newspaper advertisement for *The Epic of Everest* film screenings at the New Scala Theatre. The advert promotes a "Prologue in which will appear the 7 Tibetan Lamas". *Daily Express*, 6 December 1924.

147. "The lamas at the zoo", an article in the *Children's Newspaper* which reported on the "Tibetan lamas" visit to London Zoo, "where they particularly admired the fine Bactrian camel, another visitor from Asia".

The Lamas at the Zoo

The lamas from Tibet who have been visiting London have been to see the llamas at the Zoo. They were greatly interested in all they saw at Regent's Park, where they particularly admired the fine Bactrian camel, another visitor from Asia

147

148

148. "Tibetan musicians". Members of the Everest expedition were fascinated by Tibetan dance and music, in particular Howard Somervell, who took an interest in Tibetan folk music and transcribed songs into Western musical notation. Photographed by B. Beetham during the 1924 Mount Everest Expedition.

149. "Dancers, Rongbuk Monastery". Photographed by G. L. Mallory during the 1922 Mount Everest Expedition.

149

150

150. "Tibetan wearing dancing mask". Photographed by C. J. Morris during the 1922 Mount Everest Expedition.

151. A Tibetan dancing woman. Photographed by G. L. Mallory during the 1921 Mount Everest Reconnaissance Expedition.

151

152

152. A page from a 1936 Everest album, which contained photographs of expedition members, including many Sherpas and other porters wearing their newly issued identity discs. The publicity following the 1924 expedition and film inspired other porters to join future Everest expeditions, including a young Tenzing Norgay (fourth row, fourth from left) who began taking part in expeditions from 1935 at the age of 20.

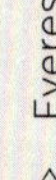

153. The iconic image of Tenzing Norgay holding his ice axe with flags of the United Nations, Great Britain, Nepal and India, following his successful summit of Mount Everest with Edmund Hillary on 29 May 1953.

153

BENTLEY BEETHAM

From the collections

At the age of 13, Bentley Beetham attended boarding school at the North Eastern County School (now called Barnard Castle School) in County Durham, England. It was here that his interest in the natural world and photography was kindled. Beetham's particular interest was ornithology, and he became one of the leading bird photographers of the day. He published several books and articles on ornithology and the conservation and protection of birds and their habitats, including *Among Our Banished Birds* (1927) and "On the position assumed by birds in flight", an article published in a volume of *British Birds* (1911). In 1914 Beetham became a teacher at his former school, teaching natural history, where he continued to share his passion for the natural world with his students until his retirement in 1949.

Beetham's interest in bird photography led him to rock climbing. He regularly climbed in the Lake District, where he met Howard Somervell, and it was this friendship which led to his invitation to join the 1924 Mount Everest Expedition. In 1919 he joined the Lake District's Fell and Rock Climbing Club and by the early 1920s he was making ascents of many Alpine peaks. Frustratingly, Beetham suffered a severe attack of sciatica during the expedition and was only able to reach Camp III. However, this misfortune allowed him to spend more time with the camera, photographing mountain scenery and camp life.

Beetham's legacy is his contribution to the photographic record of the 1924 Mount Everest Expedition, capturing important insights into the Tibetan people and their culture and the dramatic Himalayan mountain landscapes in the early twentieth century. The RGS holds approximately 1,000 of Bentley Beetham's stunning photographs within the 1924 Mount Everest Expedition photographic collection.

154

155

"He was a fine climber, a good friend, an unselfish companion and a brave one."

– T. H. Somervell, Obituary: B. Bentley Beetham, *Himalayan Journal*, vol. 24, 1963

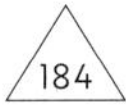

156

157

158

154. This photograph by Bentley Beetham was probably taken in the Chumbi Valley. A team member, perhaps Edward Norton or Howard Somervell, can be seen in the centre with a sketchpad and paints.

155. "Tibetan snow cocks". Beetham took many photographs of the birds and animals encountered en route to Everest.

156. A Tibetan street scene with Edward Norton in the background.

157. Tibetans. Beetham's photographs during the expedition leave an invaluable record of Tibetan life in the 1920s.

158. Beetham only reached Camp III due to sciatica. This photograph shows Camp III with Everest rising above the flank of Changtse.

AFTERWORD

by Saray N. Khumalo

My Everest Journey and the Birth of "Summits with a Purpose"

Embarking on my journey to Mount Everest was more than a personal challenge: it became a testament to the potential use of mountaineering as a force for good. My odyssey into the world of high-altitude climbing began with Mount Kilimanjaro, in Tanzania, as a bucket-list adventure, and it was a journey in 2012 that opened my eyes to the transformative power of summits and the birth of Summits with a Purpose. As part of a group of five adventurers, we not only conquered Kilimanjaro but also used the climb as an opportunity to raise funds for an orphanage in Johannesburg, setting the stage for what would become a lifelong commitment to combining my passion for climbing and adventure with a greater purpose.

The official South African team's first ascent of Everest took place in 1996, 43 years after Sir Edmund Hillary and Tenzing Norgay first reached the summit in 1953 and 72 years after the 1924 expedition. The expedition, however, was marred by tragedy when British photographer Bruce Herrod went missing during the descent of the mountain. This sombre event served as a stark reminder of the unpredictable and unforgiving nature of Everest, casting a shadow over the triumph of reaching the top and portraying the attempts as purely selfish in some quarters. This historic expedition marked a significant milestone in the history of mountaineering by Africans, not only for South Africa but also for the entire continent.

My personal journey to Everest was therefore influenced by the stories of those Africans who came before me, including South African climber Sibusiso Vilane, who was the first black man to summit Everest in 2003. Vilane's achievements were not confined to one Everest summit, as he also summited on both the North and the South side with an additional 2018 attempt without oxygen. His accomplishments, along with those of other African trailblazers such as Cathy O'Dowd, paved the way for a new generation of climbers.

I attempted to climb Everest three times – in 2014, 2015 and 2017 – before finally reaching the summit in May 2019. The first of my four Everest journeys in 2014 aimed to rewrite the narrative of African mountaineering and inspire the next generation of climbers from the continent. The pioneering effort led by Sibusiso Vilane sought to challenge stereotypes and showcase the strength and determination of African climbers and how the spirit of *ubuntu* (I am because you are) can transcend altitude, especially after the controversy surrounding the 1996 African Everest expedition.

Three key factors affected my decision when extensively researching the logistics company for my summit attempt. It should be a company:

- Underpinned by eco-friendly practices.
- Managed and owned by locals to ensure my fee would be channelled into the local community in full.
- With a good track record and yet also cost-effective.

Although I did my research before first attempting Everest in 2014, I had "romantic" ideas about Everest expeditions and what to expect on the mountain. During this first attempt, I was confronted with a world that assumed an African woman should be aiming for Everest Base Camp and no further. A world that questioned whether I was a mother and yet didn't see the need to pose the same question to fathers on the expedition. I also only encountered three people of colour on the mountain in the four to five weeks I spent in the Himalayas during that season and only a handful of women going further than Base Camp. The last revelation was that the Sherpas were also capable of rioting and demanding fair compensation for the work that they did on the mountain.

In the span of ten years, since I attempted to climb Everest for the first time in 2014, the high-altitude mountaineering landscape has changed significantly. This metamorphosis on the slopes of Everest and among the mountaineering society exemplifies a strength of resolve, a shared goal and a commitment to diversity and inclusiveness. The demographic change should be seen as a symbol of hope in the mountaineering world. It implies a common acknowledgement that the mountains belong to everyone, irrespective of sex and origin. It represents another move towards breaking down stereotypes and ensuring a fairer representation on the highest part of the world's surface.

As Everest embraces a more diverse cohort of climbers, it paves the way for a mountaineering world that is not only diverse but also truly inclusive. The mountains, once considered exclusive domains, are becoming spaces where a global community can converge, each step a stride towards a future where a love of the peaks is shared by all. This transformation is not just about conquering mountain summits; it's also about elevating the spirit of unity, resilience and the shared human endeavour to reach new heights and go beyond boundaries – both literally and metaphorically.

SELECT BIBLIOGRAPHY

Barry, I. "The Cinema: The Epic of Everest at the Scala", *Spectator*, 20 December 1924

Bruce, C. G. "Darjeeling to the Rongbuk Glacier Base Camp", *The Geographical Journal*, vol. 60, no. 6, 1922

Bruce, C. G. *The Assault on Mount Everest, 1922*, New York: Longmans, Green & Co., 1923

Bruce, C. G. *The Fight for Everest: 1924*, London: Edward Arnold & Co., 1925

Bruce, G. "The Journey Through Tibet and the Establishment of the High Camps", *The Geographical Journal*, vol. 64, no. 6, 1924

Burrard, S. G. "Mount Everest: The Story of a Long Controversy", *Nature*, vol. 71, 1904

Burrard, S. G. "The Name of Mount Everest", *Nature*, vol. 127, 1931

Cameron, I. *To the Farthest Ends of the Earth: 150 Years of World Exploration*, London: Macdonald, 1980

Carr, H. *The Irvine Diaries*, Reading: Gastons-West Col Publications, 1979

Davis, W. *Into the Silence: The Great War, Mallory and the Conquest of Everest*, London: Bodley Head, 2011

Driver, F and Jones, L. *Hidden Histories of Exploration*, Royal Holloway/RGS-IBG, 2009

Du Halde, J-B. *Description geographique historique, chronologique, politique, et physique de l'Empire de la Chine*, The Hague, 1736

Faull, J. *Climbing Mount Everest: Expeditionary Film, Geographical Science and Media Culture, 1922 – 1953*, PhD thesis, Royal Holloway, University of London, 2019

Finch, G. I. "The Second High Climb", *The Geographical Journal*, vol. 60, no. 6, 1922

Fleetwood, L. *Science on the Roof of the World: Empire and the Remaking of the Himalaya*, Cambridge: Cambridge University Press, 2022

Freshfield, D. "Exploration in the Mustagh Mountains: Discussion", *The Geographical Journal*, vol. 2, no. 4, 1893

Gillman, P. and Gillman, L. *The Wildest Dream: Mallory, His Life and Conflicting Passions*, London: Headline, 2000

Gillman, P. *Everest, 1921 to 1953: A Photographic History*, London: The Folio Society, 2021

Hammer, M. C. "Heights and Distances, Geometric Determination of", *The History of Cartography, vol. 4, Cartography in the European Enlightenment*, eds. Edney, M. H. and Pedley, M. S. Chicago: University of Chicago Press, 2020

Hansen, P. "The Dancing Lamas of Everest: Cinema, Orientalism and Anglo-Tibetan Relations in the 1920s", *American Historical Review*, vol. 101, 1996, pp.712–747

Howard-Bury, C. *Mount Everest: The Reconnaissance, 1921*, London: Edward Arnold, 1922

Howard-Bury, C. "The Mount Everest Expedition", *The Geographical Journal*, vol. 59, no. 2, 1922

Isserman, M. and Weaver, S. *Fallen Giants: A History of Himalayan Mountaineering from the Age of Empire to the Age of Extremes*, New Haven: Yale University Press, 2008

Keay, J. *The Great Arc: The Dramatic Tale of How India was Mapped and Everest Was Named*, New York: HarperCollins, 2001

Markham, C. R. *A Memoir on the Indian Surveys*, London: Sold by W. H. Allen and Co., 1878

McKay, A. *Tibet and the British Raj: The Frontier Cadre 1904–1947*, Dharmasala: Library of Tibetan Works, 2009

Noel, J. *Through Tibet to Everest, 1927* (4th edition), London: Hodder and Stoughton, 1989

Norgay, T. *Tiger of the Snows: The Autobiography of Tenzing of Everest with James Ramsey Ullman*, New York: G. P. Putnam's Sons, 1955

Norton, E. "The Mount Everest Dispatches", *The Geographical Journal*, vol. 64, no. 2, 1924

Norton, E. "The Personnel of the Expedition", *The Geographical Journal*, vol. 64, no. 6, December 1924

Norton, E. *The Fight for Everest: 1924*, London: Edward Arnold & Co., 1925

Noyce, W. *South Col: One Man's Adventure on the Ascent of Everest, 1953*, London: Heinemann, 1954

Ortner, S. *Life and Death on Mt. Everest: Sherpas and Himalayan Mountaineering*, Princeton: Princeton University Press, 1999

Probst, P. J. *The Future of the Great Game: Sir Olaf Caroe, India's Independence, and the Defense of Asia*, Akron, Ohio: University of Akron Press, 2005

Simpson, T. "Clean Out of the Map: Knowing and Doubting Space at India's High Imperial Frontiers", *History of Science*, vol. 55, no. 1, 2017

Somervell, T. H. *After Everest*, London: Hodder & Stoughton, 1936

Somervell, T. H. "Obituary: B. Bentley Beetham", *Himalayan Journal*, vol. 24, 1963

Tharkay, A. *Sherpa: The Memoir of Ang Tarka*, Seattle: Mountaineers Books, 2016

"The Mount Everest Kinematograph Film", *The Geographical Journal*, vol. 61, no. 1, 1923

Unsworth, W. *Everest* (3rd edition), London: Baton Wicks, 2000

Ward, M. "Mapping Everest", *The Cartographic Journal*, vol. 31, no. 1, 1994

Ward, M. "The Exploration and Mapping of Everest", *The Alpine Journal*, 1994

Ward, M. *Everest: A Thousand Years of Exploration. A Record of Mountaineering, Geographical Exploration, Medical Research and Mapping*, Glasgow: The Ernest Press, 2003

Younghusband, F. *The Epic of Mount Everest*, London: Edward Arnold & Co., 1926

A Note on Measurements and Spellings

When referencing heights, we have used the pre-metric measurements first as these were in common usage during the Everest expeditions of the 1920s. The height given to Mount Everest in the 1920s was 29,002 feet. This was revised on several occasions, including a height of 29,028 feet, established by the Survey of India between 1952 and 1954, which was widely accepted and used by mapping agencies and researchers. However, in 2020, both China and Nepal agreed on a new height of 29,032 feet – the height we have referred to in this book.

Place names have been given the latest anglicised versions, with occasional variations. However, quoted material, including some image captions (shown within quotation marks) have been kept in the original style and spelling.

Many of the images and archives of Everest expeditions contained within the Collections of the Royal Geographical Society (with IBG) were listed and catalogued shortly after the return of the expeditions to Britain. The text of these descriptions and captions is preserved as a source of context and information for researchers. Use of such historical terms in this book is intended for this purpose only and does not necessarily reflect the views of the Society or of mountaineers today.

INDEX

Page numbers in *italics* refer to illustrations

A

Alpine Club 42, 60, 62, 136, 172
American Alpine Club *175*
American Foundation for International Mountaineering, Exploration and Research (AFFIMER) 150
Ang Tharkay 175–6
Anville, Jean-Baptiste Bourguignon d' 18, 20, *21*

B

Bahadur, Man 14, 100, *148*
Bailey, Frederick M. 22, 43
Barry, Iris 158
Base Camp 92, *93*, 96, 100, *101*, *106*, *148*, 158
Beetham, Bentley *148*, 184–5
  1924 expedition *83*, *97*, 98, *140*, 154
  photographs by *47*, *49*, 96, *98*, *101–3*, *106*, *113*, *117*, *121*, *122*, 184–5
Bell, Sir Charles 42–3, *43*, 61
Bhavachakra *48*
Bradley, Lydia 15
British Mission to Tibet (1903–4) 14, 41, *41*, *54*
Bruce, Charles Granville 41, 62, 80, *86*, 92, 96, *133*
Bruce, Geoffrey 62, 63, *72*, 80, *82*, *83*, 96, *97*, *104*, 112, 116, 118, *124*
Buchan, John 156
Buddhism *48*, *49*
Bullock, Guy *64*
Bullock, Henry 62

C

Camp I 92, 100, 116
Camp II 92, 100
Camp III 100, *108*, *110–11*, 116, *117*, 184, *185*
Camp IV *72*, 100, 116, *122*, *123*, *137*, 138, 139, *143*, *162*, 176
Camp V 63, 118, 121, *126*, 136, 138, 139
Camp VI 118, 121, *130*, 138, 139, 150
Chandra Das, Sara *35*
Changtse *123*, *128*, *185*
Chenopo, Gana Suta 174
Chjedi, Lhakpa 116, *130*
Chomo-lung-ma (goddess) 174
Chomolungma *see* Everest
Chumbi Valley *184*
Climbing Mount Everest (film) 80, 156
clothing 132, *133*
Crawford, Colin 63
Curzon, Lord 41, 43, 60

D

Dalai Lama 22, 38, 41, 42, 43, 174
"dancing lamas" 158, 174–5
Das, Sarat Chandra 82
Dochen *66*
Dreyer, Georges 112
Driver, Professor Felix *79*
Dzatrul Rinpoche 38, *53*, *105*

E

East Rongbuk Glacier 62, 100, *107*, *109–11*, *146–7*
The Epic of Everest (film) 10, 158, *158*, *159*, *163–5*, 172, 174, *176*
equipment 112–13, 120, 132–3, 136, 140
Everest 36–55
  early expeditions 56–75
  and the frontiers of Empire 40–3
  mapping 16–35
Everest, George 20, 22, *26*
expeditions, early 56–75
  see also individual expeditions
Explorers Films 157, 176

F

film and photography 152–69
Finch, George 62, 63, *63*, *72*, 96, 98, 112, 113, *113*
First Step 121, 150
Freshfield, Douglas 18, 60

G

Gavin, Jim 82
George V, King 172
Goossens, Eugene 158
Gorang *27*, *30*
Graham, Dr J. A. 40
Great Couloir 118, 120
Great Himalayan Range 18
Great Trigonometrical Survey of India (GTS) *19*, 20, 22, *23*, *26*, 34, *34*

H

Habeler, Peter 15
Harker, Joseph 158
Hazard, John de Vars 23, 96, 98
Helps, Francis 158
Heron, Alexander 62, *64*
Herrod, Bruce 186
Hillary, Edmund 15, 176, *183*, 186
Himalayan mountain range 18
Hingston, Richard 96
Hinks, Arthur 98, 156, 159
Howard-Bury, Charles 22, 40, 58, 61, *64*, 81
  photographs by *31*, *51*, *43*, *60–1*, *66*, *67*, *168*
Hurley, Frank 143
Hussain, Syed Mir Mohsin *26*

I

Index Chart (1870) *23*
Irvine, Andrew *83*, *93*
  1924 expedition 96–99, *110–11*, *113*, 116, 120–1, *131*, *133*
  disappearance and death 14, 136–42, *146–8*, 150, 172, 174, *174*, *175*, 176

J

Jacot-Guillarmod, Charles *33*
Jelep La *102–3*
Jones, Dr Lowri *79*
Jumu Lungma Alin 20

K

Kahn, Albert 168
Kampa Dzong *47*, *54*, *55*, 62, 74, *86*, 99
Kazi, Gyalzen 80–1, *84*, 98
Kellas, Alexander 60, 62, 74–5, 78, 112, *148*
Kellas Rock Peak *107*
Khan, Abdul Jalil 23, 82
Khartaphu *146–7*
Khumalo, Saray 15

L

Lagay *27*, *30*
Lambert, Raymond 15
Lambton, William 20, 22, *26*
Lambton's Great Arc 22, *23*
Lambton's Great Theodolite *26*
Lapchi Kang *65*
Lhamo, Rinchen 174
Longstaff, Tom 60, 62, 98, 112

M

Macdonald, David 40, 82
Macdonald, John 82, 83, *83*, *97*
Mallory, George *104*, *119*
  1921 expedition *39*, 58, *59*, 62, *64*, *68–9*
  1922 expedition 62, 63, *70*, *71*
  1924 expedition *83*, 96–9, 116, 118–21, *121*, *131*, 136–42, *147–8*
  disappearance and death 14, 136–42, *147–8*, 150–1, 172, 174–6
Mallory, Ruth 98, 119, 120, *149*
Mallory and Irvine Research Expedition 15, 150
mani stones *49*
mapping Everest 16–35

Markham, Clements 20
Messner, Reinhold 15, 176
Miyolangsangma 40
Montgomerie, Thomas 34
Morley, John 60, 61
Morris, Charles John 38, *53*, *81*, 172
Morshead, Henry 18, *19*, 22, 62, *64*
Moti *85*, 98
Mount Everest Committee (MEC) 61, 62, 96, 98, 132, 154, 156, 159, 172
Mount Everest Expedition (1922) 14, 62–3, 96, 120
  photographs from *53*, *70–3*, *81*, *85*, *86*, 156, *169*, *179*, *180*
Mount Everest Expedition (1924) 14, 23, 92, 94–113, 184
  film and photography 152–69
  final approach 114–33
  legacy of 170–87
  loss of Mallory and Irvine 134–51
  photographs from *32*, *47*, *48*, *50*, *52*, 82, *83*, *88*, *91*, *93*, *178*
  Sherpas 78, 116, 118, *160*, *161*, *164–5*, 175, *175*
Mount Everest Expedition (1933) 14, 150
Mount Everest Expedition (1935) 14
Mount Everest Expedition (1936) 14, *90*, *91*, *182*
Mount Everest Expedition (1938) 15
Mount Everest Expedition (1953) 15, *183*
Mount Everest Reconnaissance Expedition (1921) 14, *27*, 42–3, 58, 61–2, 63, 74, 81, 112, 120
  photographs from *19*, *30*, *31*, *33*, *39*, *46*, *51*, *60–1*, *64*, *65*, *84*, *112*, *113*, *181*
Mount Everest Reconnaissance Expedition (1951) 15
Murchison, Sir Roderick 22

N
Noel, John 38, 61, 74, *92*, *121*
  1922 expedition *70*, *79*, *87*, *113*, 154
  1924 expedition *48*, *50*, *52*, 62, *83*, *88*, 96, *97*, *104*, *107*, *109*, 121, *123*, *124*, *144*, *145*, 154, *155*, 156–69
  Climbing Mount Everest 80
  The Epic of Everest 172, 174, *176*
Noel, Sybille 158
Norgay, Tenzing 14, 15, 78, 80, 82, 175–6, *182*, *183*, 186
North Col *11*, *13*, 14, *60–1*, *68–9*, *73*, *79*, 100, 116, 118, 119, *122–3*, *128*, 139, *162*
North Face 96, *106*, 116, *117*, 118–21
North Peak *60–1*, *68–9*
North Ridge 118, 120, 121
Northeast Ridge *71*, 120–1, 136
Norton, Edward *104*, *119*
  1922 expedition 62, 63, *71*
  1924 expedition 78, *83*, 92, 96, *97*, 100, *101*, 116–20, *124–30*, 136, *137*, *146–7*, 150
Noyce, Wilfred 176

O
Odell, Noel *105*
  1924 expedition *83*, *93*, 96, *97*, 98, *99*, *113*, 116, 119–21, *131*, 136–41, *142*, *147*, 150
O'Dowd, Cathy 186
oxygen 15, 112–13, 120, 136, 140

P
Paro Jong *55*
Pasang, Ang *27*, *30*
Pasang, Dorjay 116
Pathé News 157
Pauhunri 60, 74, *75*
Paul, Karma *55*, 62, 78, 80, 81–3, *86*, *90*, *91*, *93*, 98
Pereira, Arthur 157
Ponting, Herbert 143, 156
Pumori, Mount *124–5*, *127*
pundits 34, *34–5*

R
Raeburn, Harold 62, *64*
Raetz, Alfred 159, 168
Ram, Hari 22
Rawling, Cecil G. 22
Rennell, James 20
Rennick, Major *55*
Rhombu 98
Rongbuk Glacier 96, *106*, *124–5*
Rongbuk Monastery 38, *52*, *53*, 62, 80, 100, *101*, *105*, *169*, 172, *179*
Royal Geographical Society (RGS) 42, 58, 60, 74, 172
  Founder's Medal *35*
  "Hidden Histories of Exploration" *79*
Ruttledge, Hugh 150
Ryder, Charles Henry Dudley 22

S
Sagarmatha *see* Everest
Second Step 121, 150
Semchumbi 116, *130*
Shamsherpun, Lance-Naik 14, 100, *148*
Shaw, George Bernard 119
Shebbeare, Edward *83*, 96, *97*
Shekar Monastery *50*, *51*, *67*, *169*
Sherpas 40, 74, *74*, 76–93
  1921 expedition 62
  1922 expedition 14, 63, *73*, *122*, *148*, 172
  1924 expedition 78, 116, 118, *160*, *161*, *164–5*, 175, *175*
  "Tigers" 78, *88*, 116, *130*
Sikdar, Radhanath 22, 58
Simla Convention (1914) 42
Simonsen, Eric 150
Singh, Gujjar 18, *19*, 22, 62, 82
Singh, Kishen (A-K) 34, *34*
Singh, Nain 34, *34*, *35*
Singh, Turubaj 22
Singh Milamwal, Rai Bahadur Kishen *35*
Singh Sahi, Jemadar Lachiman *91*
Singh Thapa, Hari 23, *32*, *33*
Smythe, F. S. *91*
Somervell, Howard 58, 82, *178*, 184
  1922 expedition 62, 63, *71*, *73*
  1924 expedition *83*, 96, *97*, *108*, 116, 118–19, *119*, *124–30*, *148*, 154
South Peak *68–9*
Spencer, Sydney 98
sponsorship deals 132
summit *126*, *145*, *155*
Summits with a Purpose 186–7
supplies 132–3
Swiss Mount Everest Expedition (1952) 15

T
Tabei, Junko 15
Taktsang *54*
Tashi, Lobsang 116
Tejbir Bura, Lans-Naik 63, *72*, 82, *82*
Thapa, Lalbir Singh 22, 62, 82
Through Tibet to Everest 167
Tibetan Plateau *43*, 99, 158
"Tigers" 78, *88*, 116, *130*
timeline 14–15
The Tragedy of Everest 159, *166*
Trisul 60, 112
Tsarong Dzasa 43
Tsering, Lhakpa 116, 174

U
Ugyen Wang Chuk, Sir *55*
Unna, P. J. H. 112

V
Vilane, Sibusiso 15, 186

W
Waddell, L. A. *25*
Wakefield, Arthur *72*
Wang Hong-Bao 150
Wangdi, Chhetan 80–1, *84*
Ward, Michael 22
Waugh, Andrew 22, *24*, 58
Weatherall, V. E. 92
Wheeler, Edward O. 18, 22, *27*, *30*, *33*, 62, *64*
White, John Claude 54–5, *55*
Windy Col Camp *60–1*
Winthrop Young, Geoffrey *149*
Wollaston, Alexander Frederick Richmond 38, *46*, 62, *64*, *65*
Wood, Henry 22
Wyn-Harris, Percy *91*, 150

Y
Yashimoro, Hasegawa Ryoten 150
Yellow Band 118
Yishe, Norbu 116, *130*
Younghusband, Sir Francis 14, 22, 40, 41, 54, 58

Acknowledgements

The Royal Geographical Society (with IBG) would like to thank the authors – Dr Katherine Parker, Dr Jonathan Westaway, Eugene Rae, Professor Felix Driver, Peter Gillman, Dr Jan Faull and Dr Peter H. Hansen – for their contributions to the book. The Society is indebted to them for their meticulous scholarship on the early Everest expeditions. We would like to give special thanks to Felix Driver for his guidance and advice during this project.

Notes on contributors

Professor Felix Driver, Royal Holloway, University of London, is a historical geographer specializing in collections-based research and public engagement in the arts and humanities.

Dr Jan Faull, former Archive Production Curator at the British Film Institute, recently completed a PhD at Royal Holloway, University of London, on expeditionary films and media culture.

Peter Gillman is an Everest author, editor and biographer, and co-winner, with his wife Leni Gillman, of the Boardman Tasker Award for Mountain Literature in 2000.

Professor Peter H. Hansen is Professor of History and Director of International and Global Studies at Worcester Polytechnic Institute, Massachusetts.

Saray Khumalo is a mountaineer, speaker, transformation coach and the first black African woman to summit Mount Everest and ski to the South Pole.

Dr Katherine Parker is Cartographic Collections Manager for the Royal Geographical Society (with IBG).

Eugene Rae is Principal Librarian at the Royal Geographical Society (with IBG).

The Royal Geographical Society (with IBG) is indebted to Norbu Tenzing for his insight into the historical legacy of these expeditions and his work highlighting the environmental and social impact of Himalayan mountaineering today.

Dr Jonathan Westaway, University of Central Lancashire, is a Senior Research Fellow specializing in the history of mountaineering, mountain environments and imperial cultures of exploration.